Advance Praise for

START-UP CITY

"Cities are leading the change in America. *Start-Up City* gives a window into how to align all of the stars to make it happen. Gabe's playbook provides an inside look at how to integrate private-sector skills and processes while instituting strong, public-oriented management and governance. *Start-Up City* is a must read for anyone interested in making positive change in our cities."

—RAY LAHOOD, former United States Secretary of Transportation

"Gabe shows us the art of the possible. This book is not just another lofty call to build more livable cities. It is a practical guide on how to put people first in cities and how to move quickly from idea to execution."

—CAROL COLETTA, VP/Community and National Initiatives, The John S. and James L. Knight Foundation

"Adaptation, innovation, and a commitment to getting sh*t done fast aren't management strategies limited to the private-sector boardroom. Investment in our cities is mission critical for our future, and *Start-Up City* identifies a new urban entrepreneurialism in the public interest."

—JANETTE SADIK-KHAN, Bloomberg Associates; former NYC DOT Commissioner

"Gabe's lessons in *Start-Up City* break down the barriers between the public and private sectors in pursuit of a greater city and citizenry. The elusive recipe for successfully innovating within the confines of government is in this book."

—ADRIAN FENTY, former Mayor of the District of Columbia

"*Start-Up City* challenges cities to be more nimble and shows them how. Gabe outlines fixes for the disconnect between cities and the private sector. He mixes the simplicity of bike lanes and the wizardry of self-guiding cars with the sharing economy to paint a new picture of mobility. He brings an impish humor to the serious business of change. City-lovers everywhere should read this book."

—MARTHA ROSKOWSKI, Vice President of Local Innovation, PeopleForBikes

"Finally—the missing manual for the vanguard of can-do change agents who have discovered in their cities a once-in-a-generation opportunity to make a real, lasting impact on American government. What Gabe Klein has learned transforming transportation in D.C. and Chicago will be invaluable as future young leaders take on housing, health care, and other once-intractable urban challenges."

—ANTHONY TOWNSEND, author of *Smart Cities*

"It is amazing that D.C. and Chicago gave entrepreneur outsider Gabe Klein the keys to the transportation bus. Now, in *Start-Up City,* he pulls lessons from the thrilling ride. Klein's disruptive wisdom extracts management, communication, and finance advice from potholes, bike share, and a suite of innovative projects for change-makers inside and outside city hall. Klein muses on a future impacted by cars that drive themselves, but more importantly, advises how to steer that future toward the city we want to live in soon."

—RANDY NEUFELD, Director, SRAM Cycling Fund

About Island Press

Since 1984, the nonprofit organization Island Press has been stimulating, shaping, and communicating ideas that are essential for solving environmental problems worldwide. With more than 1,000 titles in print and some 30 new releases each year, we are the nation's leading publisher on environmental issues. We identify innovative thinkers and emerging trends in the environmental field. We work with world-renowned experts and authors to develop cross-disciplinary solutions to environmental challenges.

Island Press designs and executes educational campaigns in conjunction with our authors to communicate their critical messages in print, in person, and online using the latest technologies, innovative programs, and the media. Our goal is to reach targeted audiences—scientists, policymakers, environmental advocates, urban planners, the media, and concerned citizens—with information that can be used to create the framework for long-term ecological health and human well-being.

Island Press gratefully acknowledges major support of our work by The Agua Fund, The Andrew W. Mellon Foundation, The Bobolink Foundation, Center for the Living City, The Curtis and Edith Munson Foundation, Forrest C. and Frances H. Lattner Foundation, The JPB Foundation, The Kresge Foundation, The Oram Foundation, Inc., The Overbrook Foundation, The S.D. Bechtel, Jr. Foundation, The Summit Charitable Foundation, Inc., and many other generous supporters.

The opinions expressed in this book are those of the author(s) and do not necessarily reflect the views of our supporters.

START-UP
CITY

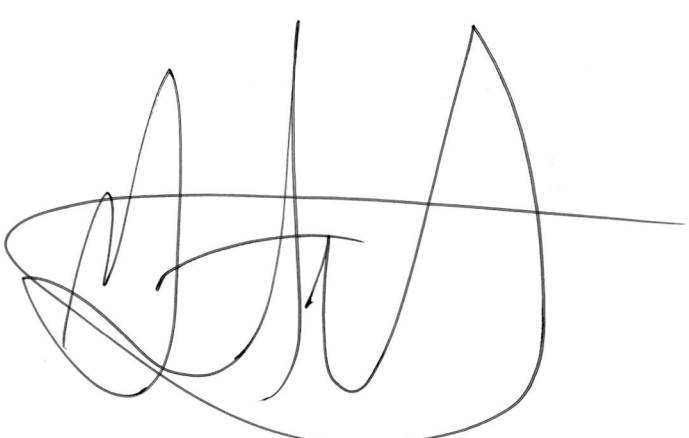

START

Gabe Klein

with David Vega-Barachowitz

Foreword by Robin Chase

Inspiring Private &
Public Entrepreneurship,
Getting Projects Done,
and Having Fun

UP

CITY

 **ISLAND**PRESS | Washington | Covelo | London

Island Press is a trademark of The Center for Resource Economics.

This project was made possible with the support of the John S. and James L. Knight Foundation.

Library of Congress Control Number:
2015941185

Printed on recycled, acid-free paper ♳

Manufactured in the United States of America
10 9 8 7 6 5 4 3

Keywords: autonomous vehicle, bike lanes, bike share, entrepreneurship, participatory government, public participation, public-private collaboration, public-private partnership, Six Sigma, social marketing, S.M.A.R.T, technological innovation

For Stephanie and Simone

Contents

Foreword

Way back at the end of 2002, I hired Gabe to creatively run our fledgling Zipcar office in Washington, D.C. The car-sharing company was young and lean. Our customers were the center of our universe. We were blazing a new path in a long-established and rigid environment. Everyone perceived the transport sector to consist of large-scale infrastructure projects all requiring years of planning, analysis, and high (and low) finance—a realm for civil engineers and bureaucrats. Creating desirable, sexy, consumer-facing products was in the jurisdiction of car companies, who themselves were hardly sprightly, requiring five to eight years to bring a vehicle to market. Innovation—fast-paced or not—was never something associated with the transport sector. This was new ground that Zipcar was breaking.

Six years later, when Gabe was hired to be D.C.'s director of transportation, I was excited for the city, but also skeptical. Gabe would bring to D.C. a focus on meeting residents' needs with a wholly open mind, unhindered by whatever wisdom was the status quo in city government. I also wondered how he would ever manage to get anything done in that big soup of rules, regulations, power structures, and plodding workforce that I imagined cities to be. Furthermore, what did Gabe know about working in a big, entrenched bureaucracy?

This book is that answer.

Gabe somehow had the intuition, the common sense, the political skill, the charisma, and the chutzpah to not only get things done, but to get them done quickly and done well. He knows that to make change, you cannot go it alone. He did it together with his team; together with the help of other departments; together with the engagement of the private sector, and together with the buy-in and support of residents. Now that's a trick. And he did it twice (hello, Chicago!).

Gabe has understood that cities, much like startups, need to make sure that they leave room for experimentation, learning, adaptation, and ongoing evolution. In fact, cities need to plan for this dynamic learning process. Cities need to assess their strengths and assets so they can effectively partner with the private sector and leverage what individual citizens do best in terms of systems, execution, innovation, creativity, and hyperlocalization. Gabe describes how large-scale change should be conceived, and then how it can be done. No more, no less.

Start-Up City is a helpful guide steeped in pragmatic realism. Cities must succeed, and they must become the foundation for thriving lives. With a burgeoning 7.5 billion people on the planet, this is humanity's only way forward. Gabe's book helps make that future possible. And we need to start now.

ROBIN CHASE is cofounder and former CEO of Zipcar, founder of Veniam, and author of *Peers Inc.: How People and Platforms are Inventing the Collaborative Economy and Reinventing Capitalism.*

Preface

Building a New Chicago (Arvell Dorsey, Jr.)

had little idea of what I was walking into when Chicago mayor Rahm Emanuel recruited me as his transportation commissioner. I had visited Chicago twice for a total of only two days (and never in winter), never read *The Devil in the White City,* or even tasted a Chicago-style hot dog.

At our first meeting at his house in Washington, D.C., Rahm worked me like a true political operative. "Gabe, I'm sorry I am a few minutes late," he said. "I was having lunch with the president, and I left him to come meet you." Rahm is a master of politics, working a room and connecting eye to eye with people over the most minute issue. We spent hours talking about everything from yoga to transportation policy, finding common ground in our shared impatience for bureaucratic inertia and our mutual drive to see real transformation quickly. I was sold.

When I arrived in Chicago, I set out to accomplish a lot of things that I will elaborate on later in this book, but the future mayor and I connected on the ideas of treating constituents like customers and communicating our policies and actions proactively. I worked up a simple marketing program to connect the dots for Chicagoans, based on a similar effort I had led at Zipcar back in 2004. Just as the now familiar "Zipcars Live Here" signs in cities told customers where the Zipcars could be found in their neighborhoods, in Chicago, we made a sign for every taxpayer-funded project. The signs read "Building A New Chicago." Once I pitched the concept and worked up the basic graphics, the mayor himself supervised the ultimate layout, slogan, and even the subtitle.

After launching the program, I decided to make a second, blunter version of the sign to hang in my office. My version read simply: "Getting Sh*t Done." Each day, I reminded myself of what the mayor would really say behind closed doors, and what our actual goal in the new administration was—to serve the people of Chicago, and fast. The sign, which hung in my office for the entire time I served as transportation commissioner, remains the slogan of my tenure there.

Gabe Klein "Getting Sh*t Done" in Chicago (Gabe Klein)

Chicago, like most American cities, had a room chock-full of old plans. With dusty, yellowing pages, most of these plans were decades old and often bore witness to some of the great, unrealized ambitions of my predecessors. I remember surveying the Chicago Department of Transportation (CDOT) archives during my first week. There was a plan for a light-rail project from the 1990s quashed by the sitting governor; a plan for the Bloomingdale Trail dating back to 1998; and an ambitious, but largely unimplemented, bike plan from 1992 entitled *The Bike 2000 Plan: A Plan to Make Chicago Bicycle-Friendly by the Year 2000*. We still had a long way to go. Each of these had become stale reminders of how bureaucracy fails itself and its citizens. Today, many of these projects would cost three to four times as much to complete, but due to a lack of political will or foresight or both, all of the social and economic benefits are encapsulated in spiral-bound books collecting dust in the CDOT library.

We can talk, we can plan, we can talk some more, we can shelve a plan, and we can create new plans, but if you don't get it done, then it didn't happen, right? This is no slight to the planning field—quite the opposite. It's a recognition that moving quickly from conception to planning to engineering to building is hard. Implementation is painful. It's also true that planning is an important exercise, and not every idea should be taken to fruition. But it is possible to get things done quickly, even as you trudge through the bureaucratic sludge of city government. If I didn't see my work implemented (or at least construction started) during my (or my boss's) tenure, I felt a sense of failure, and ultimately, so will the people you serve.

There are a couple reasons to be obsessed with speed of implementation. The primary reason—and why I wanted to write this book—is that we have no time to waste. With seemingly insurmountable environmental problems created just since the Industrial Revolution, compounded by an ever-expanding population, and a culture that accepts an unacceptable death rate on our streets, the time to act is *now*.

Also, we need to be realistic about political time frames. The first year a mayor is in office is the best time to strike with a public- or private-sector innovation in your city. By the fourth year, lame-duck syndrome can set in, and/or it's all about re-election. If you want to get it done, time frame is key or you may lose support.

I also decided to write this book because of two converging trends I have seen emerge over the past several years. First, the public sector, and specifically city government, has experienced a resurgence. Led mostly by large cities such as Chicago, New York, and Washington, D.C. and a new cadre of mayors with a national profile, such as Michael Bloomberg, Cory Booker, Adrian Fenty, and Rahm Emanuel, as well as mayors of smaller cities such as Portland, Seattle, Austin, and beyond, local governments have increasingly become the engines of innovation and experimentation in this country. In the transportation field, cities increasingly set the tone for national and state-level policies, and, in spite of far too limited resources, are delivering new and better services to their constituents. Second, the private sector, especially in the transportation arena, has ignited a trend toward consumer-oriented, on-demand, and easy-to-use mobility platforms. New technology and analytics-driven companies have sprouted to connect people and places with more flexibility, and are introducing competition with the old twentieth-century business models. Other services are springing up to provide multimodal information, helping traditional transit become more intelligible and responsive, and in the process, more efficient and consumer-friendly. Publicly led, public-private partnerships like bike sharing show that government still has the power and willingness to innovate and plays an important role in facilitating change where the private sector would not go it alone.

In spite of these trends, the chasm continues to grow between the public and private sectors on many fronts and in many places. This gulf stems broadly from divergent cultures, but also from the unmet challenges of change management, a lack of experience and knowledge about the opposite side's perspective, and a persistent skepticism of the capacity for government to efficiently serve the taxpayers.

During my career thus far, I have toed the line between the private and public sectors, imparting to each side the lessons I have learned from the other, while constantly continuing to absorb knowledge in the process. From my time as an executive with Zipcar and my efforts at starting a large food-truck company, to my tenure as transportation commissioner in Washington, D.C., and then Chicago, to being an entrepreneur again since, I have had the privilege and disappointment of seeing both the private and public sectors struggle to align their goals and ideals. My career to date has focused on bridging this divide, finding or constructing shared incentives that can become shared goals, better projects or services, and ultimately, better cities with more nimble, consumer-oriented bureaucracies.

Whether in the private or the public sector, a small or a large organization, or government or startup, my goal in this book is to demonstrate how to effect big, directional change—and how to do it fast. The city of tomorrow, and the demands of the future citizen, will not be constrained by narrow political windows and interests. We have learned over the last few years in government to *make change, or have change happen to you* (Uber, anyone?). I believe that the rate of change we will see in our cities due to exponential technological innovation over the next 5, 10, 25 years and beyond is almost inconceivable to us at this point. So the organizational alignment may get harder to achieve, not easier, and we don't have time to waste. I have written this book as a recipe for cutting through the morass and as a road map for getting real, meaningful initiatives off the ground in a one- to three-year time frame, but most of all, as a recipe for how to have fun while doing it.

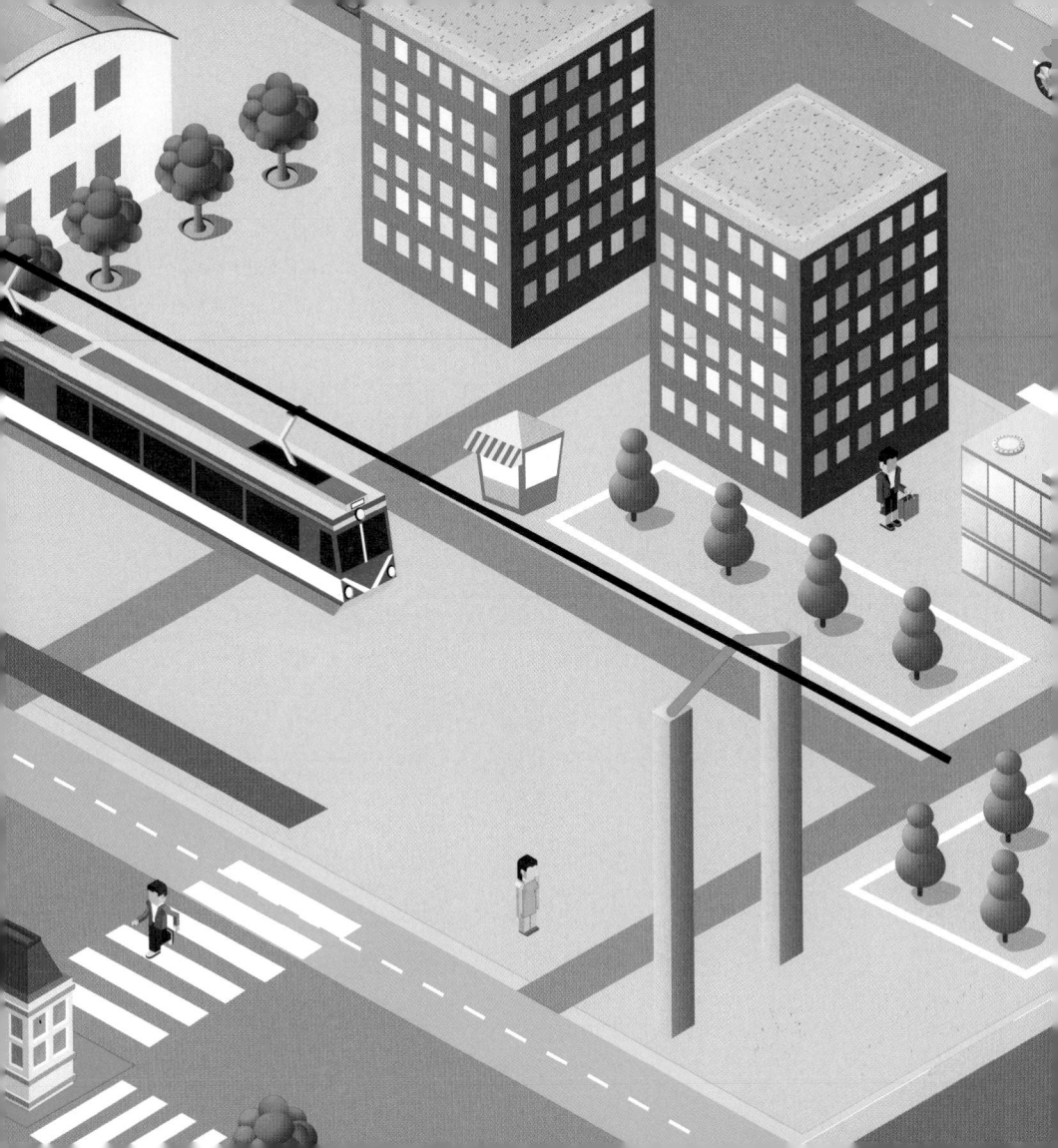

Introduction

Why Should You Care about Getting Sh*t Done in Cities?

Today's city leaders and managers face a complex web of regulatory hurdles, struggles for disparate stakeholder buy-in, risk-averse management (or politics), and funding shortages. Local governments often get the short end of the stick when budgets are slashed, even as they bear the brunt of the blame when local constituents see their services cut and their infrastructure crumble. More than ever, cities are charged with carrying out national-level policies and are expected to be at the forefront of our response to climate change, housing inequality, and public health. At the same time, most city government agencies are perennially understaffed and impeded by cumbersome, often counterproductive regulations. Seemingly insurmountable frustrations are everywhere, but you can make change in spite of these realities. If you are willing to go against the tide and follow some basic lessons in goal setting, experimentation, change management, financial innovation, and communication, you *can* get sh*t done in cities. Whether in a startup or a complex government agency, the same basic rules of management and communication apply.

The public sector needs to function much like a midsize, successful start-up, embracing the concept of cost-benefit analysis. And private companies need to use their resources and innovation skills to work for the greater good rather than just for profit. If both sides can work toward a triple-bottom-line approach within their organizations, focusing on the new P3—people, planet, profit—then the private and public spheres can meet in the middle. I believe that this is how the public-private partnerships of the future will succeed. The combative, unproductive working relationships that often characterize current government-business dynamics are anathema to building great cities and communities. Whether you are in the public, private, or nonprofit sector, you need to understand the value the other sides bring.

Managers and change makers today theoretically understand what needs to be done to make our cities more livable, sustainable, and economically viable, but have trouble practically putting together a vision and then translating that vision into implementation, never mind doing it within a one- to three-year, politically feasible time frame. As the pace of change increases, managers need to respond and lead or miss opportunities. Technology is dramatically changing the way our work is done, how we communicate information, and the business models that serve our residents. Governments need to evolve beyond the insular, silo-based cultures that are rapidly becoming outmoded in an era of exponential technological change. Otherwise, they risk reducing their own influence and relevance to serve as public policy makers and consumer advocates in a world where aggressive private industries and disruptive, consumer-savvy

Governments need to evolve beyond the insular, silo-based cultures that are rapidly becoming outmoded in an era of exponential technological change.

startups are innovating at lightning speed.

I have written this book to inspire the next generation of "public entrepreneurship," a start-up-paced energy within the public sector, brought about by leveraging the immense resources at its disposal. At the same time, we need corporate America, and start-up America, to embrace "social enterprise," working for the common good, as their primary objective versus external shareholder wealth. Combining both of these into "social entrepreneurship" allows us to move beyond public and private silos and focus on using our collective energy to solve the world's problems, regardless of your vantage point or chosen profession at the moment. To be successful in business in cities today, you need to align your goals and values as much as possible with those of city government and citizens as opposed to with profit alone. Such entrepreneurship has the potential to engender the next level of public-private partnership and give rise to new models of shared financial reward working in the interest of the greater good. Throughout this book, I will share examples of innovative and effective government, many drawn from my experiences in the Fenty administration in Washington, D.C., and the Emanuel administration in Chicago, as well as my personal experiences as an innovator and entrepreneur in business.

Through these anecdotes, project examples, and even political kerfuffles, I will lay out a road map for change, and a guide for troubleshooting the inevitable conflicts inherent to risk taking in the public sphere. I spearheaded major projects and initiatives in Chicago and Washington, D.C., that I was often told "could not be done," or "would never happen in the time frame I had planned." In proving the skeptics wrong, I became convinced that there exists a recipe for navigating the leadership challenges that span all bureaucracies. I believe that a proactive approach to partnerships between the public and private sectors should be embraced more broadly. This book will address how any individual can come into an organization, public or private, and *assess, align, set goals, finance, convince, and implement change.*

I want to encourage cross-pollination between public- and private-sector careers and dispel the myth that you need this or that training to be successful in a given area.

Who is this book for? Is it for me?

I have written this book for anyone who wants to change the way that we live in cities without waiting for the glacial pace of change in conventional government, nonprofit, or corporate settings, where the focus often remains geared toward internal politics and protecting old business models and regulatory schemes. This includes local policy makers, urban planners, urban designers, urban sustainability directors, local business leaders, entrepreneurs, employees of nongovernmental organizations (NGOs), and citizen advocates. The advent of social media has dramatically changed the interest level and participation rate of the general public in urban design and transportation projects. This has created more opportunities for the public sector to engage people and get valuable input, as well as new pressure on government to be more transparent and respond in real time.

This is absolutely not meant to be an academic text. Many people I talk to lament the academic focus of planning and public policy, with little practical focus on management and implementation. I view this work as a handbook of sorts for those who are changing careers, walking into a new job, or deciding how to have the most impact coming out of school. It's also very much a recipe for change management, even if you are in a long-standing role. I want to help prepare anyone influencing how we develop in cities to be more effective with the understanding that every situation, every job, every person, and every city is different. From my time in the public and private sectors, I recognize that there are consistent principles and approaches that span most organizations and bureaucracies, so I have worked to reference or call these out so that these lessons can apply in your world. I want to encourage cross-pollination between public- and private-sector careers and dispel the myth that you need this or that training to be successful in a given area. I happen to have a business degree, not the planning or engineering background typical for those leading government transportation agencies. If anything, this helped, not hurt, me.

How I learned about local government the hard way

Transportation directors typically come into their positions in one of three ways. (1) They move up the civil service ladder, often starting as civil engineers, and over time, assume managerial responsibilities and make major policy decisions, despite often having little formal policy background. (2) They emerge through political allegiances, often starting in the mayor's office or some other field of expertise such as public administration, and emerge in the transportation field by being well connected and politically astute. (3) They worked for a private consulting firm, often in engineering, and come in via the revolving door between the public sector and the private-sector firms, such as AECOM or CH2M Hill. There is absolutely nothing wrong with any of these paths, but I do want to point out that immediately prior to assuming the directorship at the District of Columbia Department of Transportation (DDOT), I was a food-truck entrepreneur.

Of course, at that time, there were no food trucks in most cities, and in D.C., just hot-dog trailers selling "dirty dogs" from steam trays with cloudy water. Food trucks, much like taxis, were subject to a kind of labyrinthine regulatory and licensing structure that preserves the status quo and ignores what consumers actually want. The public and the politicians mutually supported the idea of selling something beyond just hot dogs and sugar-laden soda on street corners, but the city agencies that regulated the industry had set themselves up to fail, propping up ubiquitous but low-quality services, rather than seeding entrepreneurship, creativity, and risk taking.

D.C. hot-dog cart (Don Hinchcliffe)

In 2007, after several years at Zipcar, I was ready for a change. I had long been interested in changing D.C.'s street-food scene, and like many in D.C., was frustrated at the lack of healthy and organic food options around some of D.C.'s most bustling Metro stops and public spaces. Having already built up a few public-sector relationships through Zipcar, I approached the D.C. government with an entirely new mobile food concept, which we called On the Fly. My partners and I were eager to fund the development of a fleet of customized electric food trucks, hire a four-star chef, and build a commissary for food preparation, if necessary. We wanted the government's support, permits for spaces to operate, and a regulatory climate that could foster these kinds of small businesses. After our initial meeting, the D.C. government agreed to not only explore the issue, but to make the necessary policy changes for us to operate. As a result, we invested our money and time in the business.

Line for On the Fly (Stephanie Klein)

In certain ways, the regulations and resulting state of the street-food industry at the time mirrored the same rigid regulatory structures that we have observed in other industries ripe for disruption, such as taxis. DDOT controlled the public space in which food could be sold, the Department of Consumer and Regulatory Affairs (DCRA) controlled the licensing, and the Department of Health (DOH) regulated the food preparation. DOH had only certified three commissaries for street-food preparation at that time, meaning that every single vendor on the street was linked to one of these three large warehouses. The DCRA limited the number of licenses for food vendors on the street and held a lottery for spaces. These spaces could be occupied by only one vendor at a time and for only a set number of hours. The result was "dirty dogs" for everyone. Two companies owned by a single family ran the whole enterprise because they owned the commissaries. The commissaries were more like storage facilities for carts and food, with no prep happening, because we're talking hot dogs and buns. Because they were certified by the DOH and all food prep was mandated off-cart in a commissary, any vendor basically had to work for them, and the whole business became vertically integrated, with little to no variety and a lack of true entrepreneurship. Though many of the food vendors at the time claimed to be small business owners when the competition showed up, those jobs working for the commissary owner actually offered extremely low pay—often below minimum wage—and most of the money went to the family that controlled the government-sanctioned monopoly through cart rental, services, and inflated wholesale food and drink prices.

When we entered the market, our business model was such that we wanted to follow demand—that is, the hungry masses. We balked at the idea that we would be tied to a single spot for only a few hours a day (as the current regulations insisted). Why shouldn't we go where the people go? We wanted to have trucks in the downtown squares at lunchtime and then shift to the ballgame and the clubs at night. When we explained what we were planning to the agencies in charge, their heads nearly exploded. DOH reverted to the mandated commissary model, which we were able to meet only with less-than-ideal large capital investments. DDOT and DCRA squabbled over who was in charge of what, and how to use the public space, and capitulated to the manipulation of the "hot dog mafia," as we'd come to call the family-owned commissary-vendor monopolies. Meanwhile, our company, On the Fly, was caught in the middle, because we had already plunged our own money and resources into the venture. Our investment and hard work were compromised by the intractability of government and its inability to see beyond interagency turf wars and monopolistic regulations in the interest of the common good. We survived for a few years around the Downtown D.C. Business Improvement District, where the city rules were relaxed for a few blocks, and by serving tourists on the National Mall (yes, the federal government and their partners were easier to deal with than the city government). We then had to find private space to set up our own commissary and additional private locations to operate our food trucks because so little public space was made available.

In the wake of the more recent food-truck revolution, DDOT and DCRA have developed a formal food-truck policy that mostly works. But that policy

Government had not adjusted to the concept of food trucks as mobile restaurants that shifted based on demand, favoring an archaic system whereby a license to vend was attached to a particular street space. This was designed for the immobile hot-dog-trailer monopoly and thereby eliminated creativity in food options.

Three different agencies controlled aspects of the food vending scene in D.C., and they were not necessarily communicating or in agreement. This created a nearly impossible environment for entrepreneurship.

The Street Corner Conundrum

How the Hot-Dog Cart Trumped the Food Truck at Every Turn

The Department of Health inadvertently facilitated and protected the hot-dog mafia by requiring all food vendors to store their vehicles and "make" their food in one of three commissaries owned by one family. Result = hot dogs for everyone.

(Infographic by Kate Chanba and David Vega-Barachowitz)

The D.C. Department of Regulatory Affairs controlled business licensing for food carts and trucks. The Department of Transportation regulated what spaces would be allowed for operation. Rarely did they agree. The entrepreneur was left holding the bag.

was implemented too late for us, and our venture ultimately wasn't profitable under the regulations in place at the time. Looking back on it now, especially having seen Uber and other "disruptive" businesses succeed, I think that we should have broken the rules and persevered for the public good. If we had won over consumers' appetites while breaking the rules, the rules likely would have changed. In this case, it was the dirty dogs that prevailed again, but only for a while. Today, there are more than 200 food trucks in Washington, D.C., serving fare from every continent (along with a slew of novel fusions), as well as a food-truck association to represent the industry. This makes me happy.

Me? Work in government? I had just run afoul of three city agencies, had a reputation as somewhat of an agitator in city hall, and I wouldn't be caught dead in a suit (at the time).

My experience in the food-truck business and at Zipcar had earned me a reputation in the D.C. city administrative offices as sort of a rabble-rouser. As I learned more about the necessity of understanding and shaping government policy, I joined the Greater Washington Board of Trade Transportation Policy Group around 2004. It was there that I met then-director of the DDOT Dan

Tangherlini, who was a regular speaker and presence in the group. I was the junior member of the group by at least ten years, but like Dan (who was also young), I wanted to see positive change on our streets, and we formed a lasting relationship.

In 2008, the summer after Adrian Fenty's election as mayor, I was e-mailing with Dan, who had by then taken over as D.C.'s city administrator, running day-to-day operations and guiding policy for the nation's capital. We got to talking about his successor as DDOT director. The current director was going to our beleaguered Metro transit agency as chief administrative officer after a short stint at the helm. He told me that they were in the midst of interviewing eight people from across the country to run the department, many of them typical players, but no one seemed quite right. He and Mayor Fenty wanted someone innovative, progressive, and entrepreneurial to run the agency, so he asked me if I knew anyone who fit the bill. Off the top of my head, I couldn't think of anyone, because government really wasn't my field. Three days later, I wrote Dan back and lamented that although I knew the type of combination he wanted, I could not think of a single individual that I knew of who would fit his description. Dan responded and said, "No, dummy! I was thinking of you!"

I was blown away…. Me? Work in government? I had just run afoul of three city agencies, had a reputation as somewhat of an agitator in city hall, and I wouldn't be caught dead in a suit (at the time). I thought he was joking, but I had nothing to lose and walked into city hall for my first interview in my current uniform of jeans, a short-sleeved shirt, hiking jacket, and sneakers. If I was going to work in government, I was going to do so on my own terms, and I wanted them to be aware of that from the start. I hadn't bought a suit since the '90s. Dan asked me, "Don't you own a tie?"

Making the jump from the private sector to the public sector was one of the hardest things I have ever done, but also one of the most fun and rewarding.

To my shock and surprise, they invited me back for a second interview. So I wore a dress shirt. When Dan called me a few weeks later and said he wanted me to meet with Mayor Fenty the next day, I was beginning to get cold feet. Was I really cut out for government? Would I be happy coming into work every day? It didn't feel like me, and the more I considered the reality that I had to actually buy (and wear) a new suit, the more nervous I became about the prospect of actually taking on this job. On the way to the interview, I stopped at Banana Republic and bought suit separates off the rack, ripped off the tags, and wore them out of the store to the interview a few blocks away. "I hope this was worth $300," I remember saying to myself.

Dan was clearly relieved when he saw that I had elected to wear a suit and tie for the interview with the mayor. The Fenty administration wanted someone

Left: Gabe Klein in jeans (on a Divvy bike in Chicago) (Scott Kubly)
Right: Gabe Klein in a suit (David Kidd, republished with permission © 2015 *Governing* magazine. All rights reserved.)

who could go against the grain, and when I shared some of my back story on the bike industry, Zipcar, and food trucks, the mayor and I instantly started exchanging ideas as to how to make DDOT more proactive. As I left the interview, I shook the mayor's hand and said, "I will see you this weekend, Mayor." He looked at me, surprised. "I'm catering your birthday party," I said. He smiled. As I walked out the door, I knew the job was mine if I wanted it.

During this process, President Obama had won the White House after eight years of President George W. Bush, and as an ardent follower of national politics,

We need more young entrepreneurs in government. Period.

I started to realize the size of the opportunity before me to make change. The magnitude of the challenge and the potential to collaborate at the highest levels in the nation's capital, combined with my respect for Dan and Mayor Fenty, made this a challenge I could not refuse if offered.

Mayor Fenty called me the day after Christmas in 2008 to offer me the position as director of DDOT. I took the job immediately. Hell, if it didn't work out, or if I couldn't push the envelope as much as I wanted, I would ultimately just do something else after giving it my all. Making the jump from the private sector to the public sector was one of the hardest things I have ever done, but also one of the most fun and rewarding. It is something that a lot of people who are frustrated with bureaucracy would be loathe to do, and I understand that. Working for an aggressive young mayor who was game to shake things up in an agency that had been independent for less than a decade made it more like working for a $1-billion, young company.

We need more young entrepreneurs in government. Period. It doesn't matter that you may not have a master's of public administration or a degree in urban planning and that you can't tell the DCRA from the DOT from the DOH. It's fine to be a tech start-up genius or a business school graduate working in Silicon Valley, see the myriad faults and imperfections of government, and work from the outside to be a change agent. In many cases, I actually think it's the responsible thing to do to persevere in the face of bad regulations and disrupt them. If that's what it takes to have food trucks, better taxis, or affordable accommodations, then that's what the private sector should do. But what far too few of these change agents have done is shown the courage, or taken the opportunity, to disrupt and work with these cities from within. That is a primary theme of this book and, I believe, represents the foundation of the Start-Up City.

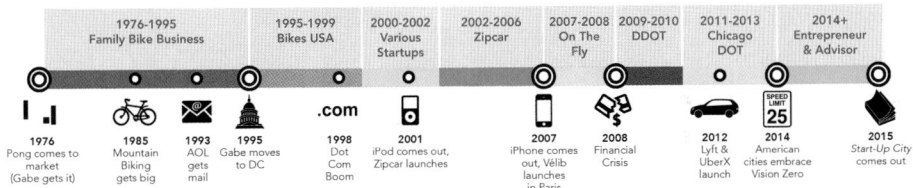

1976-1995 Family Bike Business				1995-1999 Bikes USA	2000-2002 Various Startups	2002-2006 Zipcar	2007-2008 On The Fly	2009-2010 DDOT	2011-2013 Chicago DOT		2014+ Entrepreneur & Advisor

| 1976 Pong comes to market (Gabe gets it) | 1985 Mountain Biking gets big | 1993 AOL gets mail | 1995 Gabe moves to DC | 1998 Dot Com Boom | 2001 iPod comes out, Zipcar launches | 2007 iPhone comes out, Vélib launches in Paris | 2008 Financial Crisis | 2012 Lyft & UberX launch | 2014 American cities embrace Vision Zero | 2015 Start-Up City comes out |

I'm not a linear thinker by any means, and it's important to me that this book doesn't feel like a boring timeline of my career highlights. My career, and the anecdotes that I will share with you, are intended as a device through which I can share the key principles that I believe will drive the public-private partnerships of the future. Still, I realize that jumping between years of my life, and the projects and stories therein, might be a bit disjointed. For the reader's benefit, I have included a basic timeline of my career and some of the key projects that I will reference in the book. (Infographic by Kate Chanba)

Lesson #1

(Elvert Barnes, Flickr)

Don't Be Afraid to Screw Up and Learn

It is necessary to make mistakes. Just make them as quickly as possible, learn from them, and try not to repeat.

When I was announced as director early on New Year's Eve at the DDOT headquarters with the mayor and D.C. press present, it seemed as if the whole of the agency was standing on the balconies overlooking the atrium. Even as I gave my opening speech, I could sense the skepticism amongst some in the crowd of transportation employees. Who was this smart aleck from the private sector they'd brought in to shake things up? Why did things need to change?

When the announcement came to a close and the DDOT ranks began to form a line to shake hands with their new director, a middle-aged woman with a familiar face approached. She held a firm regulatory grip in her role as program manager for public space for DDOT and had proven to be somewhat of a nemesis while my food-truck company, On the Fly, struggled to survive on the streets of Washington.

"Should I just pack up my desk now?" she asked half-jokingly under her breath as she shook my hand.

"Absolutely not," I said. "I'm going to make you my food-truck czar." I smiled, half serious.

This person wasn't the problem, but her approach was symptomatic of an ingrained culture of risk aversion and an antagonistic attitude toward the private sector. I knew that something, probably a lot of things, had to change at DDOT, and that her actions were a partial reflection of issues throughout the agency, and government as a whole.

For the next few years, I worked with this manager and many of the others in the agency to change not only their attitude about their sometimes adversarial role in relation to the public and businesses, but also to set a new open-minded tone internally and externally for their teams, and their teams' teams, as they interacted with the public.

Within the first few weeks, I took stock of a few fundamental problems at DDOT:

- Saying "yes" meant more work, especially in an era of dwindling resources. This meant that there was very little incentive to innovate or to say "yes" when someone within the agency, or a customer of the agency, wanted to do something different from the status quo.
- Stepping out on a limb meant increasing risk of failure. The aversion to failure was unlike anything I had seen before, and, as I learned later, was actually even higher in many other cities.

- There was a prevailing attitude that businesses and the private sector in general were "on the other side" and were exploiting our city resources for personal gain. All businesses—small or large—were seen as the same by many managers.
- Government defaulted to a black box and was often opaque and uncommunicative in general, and especially when project problems became public or convoluted.

I was taught to iterate and fail fast as a survival instinct in business.

This last issue surprised me. If I was going to try to sell change to the public, how could we resist giving information to people? It just wouldn't work. But this was the standard way that things were done at DDOT, and at many government agencies. Right off the bat, I realized that the best effort that I could make would be to lead by example: the director of the agency, like the mayor, sets the tone for embracing change and risk. I personally had to show that I was willing to embrace the future now and take on risk. Otherwise, we would never accomplish anything and would be stuck in a cycle of uninspiring, incremental change.

In the start-up world, "failure is not only invoked, but celebrated."

Coming from the start-up world, the idea that I was supposed to be risk averse and instinctively say "no" made no intuitive sense to me. I was taught to iterate and fail fast as a survival instinct in business. We never would have ended up with convertibles or pickup trucks at Zipcar without this philosophy. In the start-up world, "failure is not only invoked, but celebrated."[1] This has been a basic tenet of technology startups for decades. In Walter Isaacson's book on Steve Jobs, he tells the story of the iPhone launch event, where the thing literally did not work and was sporadic at best, an amalgam of iPod, phone, and computer, with nothing quite functioning as it should, even minutes before the event. Jobs held the unveiling anyway, and miraculously, when he made that first call from the stage, it went through. If he had given up because the product at that time was unreliable and a borderline failure, where would Apple be now?

So I set the expectation that we were going to experiment, make mistakes, and then make more responsible long-term decisions for the taxpayers as a result. This became the new modus operandi and freed up our teams to take risks.

My first week on the job, I went to work meeting with stakeholders inside and outside of local government in D.C., as well as in other big cities. Mayor

Fenty had spent time in New York City meeting with Mayor Bloomberg, and emulated quite a few things he learned there. He mimicked Bloomberg's bullpen office layout, in which he sat in an open cubicle with all of the mayoral staff, setting a dramatically different tone for government business (cobwebs literally grew in his sixth-floor official office, he used it so little).

New York City was doing the most interesting public space and active transportation projects in the nation at that time, and had one of the most progressive and energized teams. I met Janette Sadik-Khan, Mayor Bloomberg's transportation commissioner, at the end of 2008. Janette had already made a name for herself as a change agent by making much of Times Square into a pedestrian zone. Janette and I shared a lot of ideas, both during this meeting and after, but perhaps the most important thing she told me was to think of many of our projects as "pilots," if not in name then by approach. This strategy of experimentation and trial-and-error resonated with me. Moreover, it was cost-effective, because we could use cheap materials and fast action by internal teams to show a project's worth and build a constituency, and then find the funds to make it permanent later on. This also meshed perfectly with my "fail fast" start-up philosophy, and also with my life philosophy more broadly: It's okay to make mistakes, just make them as quickly as possible and learn from them. We also discussed the importance of documenting your work and publicly stating your goals in a way that government traditionally shied away from: short-term, milestone-based targets to measure against. Again, this was a perfect fit with the private-sector yearly strategic and budget plans that I was used to.

Mayor Adrian Fenty and Gabe Klein at a ribbon cutting. (Vikrum Dave Aiyer)

As a new guy with no experience in government, planning, or engineering, I set about asking a lot of questions, many of them "dumb" questions that would have seemed obvious to anyone who had spent time in municipal transportation. I got different reactions from people. The technical "experts" gave me an eye roll and must have thought, "Who hired this guy who doesn't even understand the federal funding formulas?" Others were delighted at the prospect of a refreshing, energized, and youthful director who didn't mind baring his lack of knowledge about the bureaucracy he had walked into, but was also asking everyone for input on his agenda. I had hundreds of conversations, with my assistants, the heads of the divisions, and everyone in between, asking, "What do you think is important that we do, that we don't currently do?" I gathered small groups that cut across the agency and presented my rapidly growing vision for the next two years. People seemed to really appreciate being heard as well as the idea of increasing the pace of change. When I started talking to people about the detriment of saying "no" to new ideas and instead encouraging staff, and the public, to float any idea they saw as worthwhile, I got a bifurcated response: excitement at this attitude from the planning group and the communications and government relations folks, and then an "ugh" from the engineers and civil technicians. I knew that some of the best ideas were going to come from laypeople, those who live, work, and play in their own neighborhood. We needed to engage and empower them.

The combination of trying new ideas, failing fast, and doing low-cost pilot projects was a lot for some people to stomach, even for me as I tried to learn all of the government protocols. In my first few months, I bungled a few things (following my own philosophy as much as possible). At one point, shortly after starting, I accidentally contradicted the mayor in the *Washington Post* regarding the funding of late-night Metro subway service from the Washington Nationals stadium. In hindsight, this mistake wasn't that big a deal, but at the time, it felt like a critical error. The mayor called me. I apologized profusely for not paying attention to his stated policy and told him it would not happen again. He responded, "All that matters is that you are willing to take responsibility for a mistake and move forward." When your boss has your back, it gives you the freedom to take risks and experiment more boldly. My boss's great example reinforced my own resolve to experiment.

Richard Branson, in his autobiography, *Losing My Virginity*, tells a great story about the redesign of the interior of the Virgin Atlantic fleet in the 1990s. When Virgin started installing the new interiors on the planes, a host of design problems surfaced, the sum of which cost Virgin millions of dollars as they struggled to salvage the overhaul. However, instead of firing the designer responsible for the snafu, Branson did just the opposite. He asked the same person to design the interior again, and this time, to succeed and prove himself. The designer did just that, and the resulting interior proved to be a seminal, award-winning design, as well as one that could have been carried out only by an eternally grateful, loyal employee hell-bent on salvaging his own reputation.

> **I knew that some of the best ideas were going to come from laypeople . . . We needed to engage and empower them.**

Learning the hard way:
The Pennsylvania Avenue bike lanes snafu

There are, unfortunately, times in management when you must assert your leadership by altering a design, critiquing a plan, or prodding your staff to do more by elevating expectations. Yet most often, whether you are the manager or the managed, such errors and misgivings provide opportunities for teachable moments.

Shortly into the first year of my tenure as DDOT director, I heeded a challenge put forth to me by Rep. Earl Blumenauer of Portland, Oregon. A stalwart of the sustainable transportation field for decades, Blumenauer had long fantasized about a bike lane on Pennsylvania Avenue in Washington, D.C., between the White House and the U.S. Capitol, and the national and local statement that it would make about the importance of active transportation.

As a student of history who was also working on the streetcar system vision and plan for Washington, D.C., I knew that the middle of Pennsylvania Avenue had once carried a streetcar line. This was, in fact, the last streetcar to run in Washington, D.C., before it shut down in 1962. In the original 1791 plan for the District by Pierre L'Enfant, the avenue had been designed as a grand boulevard with a park running along its center. This and many other proposals had gone unrealized (or been erased), leaving, in the wake of the streetcar's removal, an asphalt expanse commonly used as a staging ground for government vehicles.

Pennsylvania Avenue wasn't ideal for conventional bike lanes. There were constant right turns and poor sight lines, and the overall width of the street

The bike lanes went in on Pennsylvania Avenue where the streetcar lines historically had been (shown here in 1919). (Ken Booth/Shorpy)

made cyclists along the curb feel exposed. Although traditional bike lanes proved inadequate in concept, the center median presented an intriguing possibility for experimentation. Not one of the engineers said, "It can't be done." So we went forward with the project full speed.

I consulted Mayor Fenty on the project early on. He said that he was fine with the lanes in concept as long as they were safe and aesthetically suited

Pennsylvania Avenue's stature as a grand boulevard. He embraced the idea of using the empty space in the middle that once housed the streetcar. Over the course of several months, we met internally with our bike lane task force that crosscut the agency and had planners and engineers working together to further develop this and other bike lane projects. I made regular appearances at these weekly meetings to reinforce the importance of Pennsylvania Avenue, monitor progress, and make sure that the engineers were saying "how" instead of "no."

With my broad portfolio of projects, including the 11th Street bridges, myriad streetscapes, and a new D.C. streetcar, I took my eye off the ball for a month or so as the bike lanes reached final design. Our staff and consultants had finalized the engineering and were ready to go into construction. The last I had looked at the schematic, we were 80 percent of the way there and everything looked fine.

There are many lessons to be learned from this project, and the first is to regularly check in on major milestones with your team. I failed to see the design decisions at 90 percent and 100 percent completion, and I paid the price for my mistake.

As the crews started scraping up the old markings and setting down the new ones along the first three-block segment, I received an urgent call from the city administrator. Something didn't look right with the new bike lanes. He told me to come down to see it ASAP. Then Mayor Fenty called me and said, "Director, I don't think this is what we talked about, you need to come down here and see what they are doing." I called the team, told them to stop, and went down to the site, the United States' "Champs Élysées," and the center of the universe for American politics.

To my horror, the design being applied to the street looked completely different than what I had last seen, and instead of taking the center median as had

The botched Pennsylvania Avenue bike lanes (Stephen Davis)

been agreed upon, the engineers left this space empty, and instead took one travel lane on either side of the median space. I was mortified. I had unintentionally deceived my boss and all of our other stakeholders, including those at the federal level. Worse, these bike lanes were completely unsafe and obtrusive. Why? Drivers were instinctively driving down the auto lane–width bike lanes, which could hardly be differentiated from the travel lanes that were there beforehand. How could this have possibly happened!?

By the time I called the crews to stop working, they had already striped three blocks of the avenue and the blowback was coming. Taxi drivers, AAA, reporters, and council members in the Wilson Building were all asking, "What the hell is this, Gabe?" They had caught me with my pants so far down that I broke a cardinal rule: I tried to defend DDOT and the current design to the mayor, the city administrator, and others, rather than admit my lack of oversight and move on right away.

So what had happened? As best as I can tell, the consultant designer/engineers, our planners, and our traffic engineers had a massive groupthink lapse. While I had been preoccupied with other projects, they had reverted back to an earlier idea, and what they knew versus what was possible, convincing themselves and each other that this was the better way to do the project. I failed as a leader by neglecting to check their work when I knew I should have on such a highly visible and symbolic project. As built, the design was politically untenable, aesthetically inadequate, and to the average rider, patently unsafe, even though this was the primary objective of the project.

Sometimes things look one way on paper, or work from a technical standpoint, but prove disastrous when implemented. Laypeople, those without the credentials or the signatures or the jargon, often catch these fatal flaws immediately on sight. In this case, our team, fearing the unprecedented, had taken two travel lanes and turned them into bike lanes at close to the same width, rather than reusing the median as a center path. Cars didn't know what to do, bicyclists were overexposed, and the median—the ingenious centerpiece of the project—remained conspicuously empty, still as hollow as the day the streetcars had been removed in the early sixties.

The mayor was concerned about the botched design and rollout, but I found out from Neil Albert, the current city administrator, that Mayor Fenty was equally concerned about bursting my creative bubble and dampening my enthusiasm. Here I had defended the failed design, even after he'd given me the creative freedom to carry it out with little oversight. Now I was blown away by his empathy as a boss, even with my poor handling of our mistakes. But there was no time to reflect. Rumors were flying among advocates and bloggers that the mayor had stopped the project in its tracks. The Pennsylvania Avenue bike lanes were news—and a growing embarrassment instead of the great story they should have been. Facing the media and the politics and all of these mistakes, I did what any transportation director with no planning or engineering degree would do—I personally began redesigning it on the street, in real time, with my deputy director, Terry Bellamy, and our team that had put together the original design. We had to scrape up the brand new thermoplastic markings that we had just put down and move everything into the central median as originally planned.

I slowly backtracked with a very patient mayor and assured his team that we would fix it expeditiously. The mayor's office had our back with the press and constituents. Then we hit a second roadblock. The consultant engineer on the project adamantly refused to sign off on the redesign, meaning that the project lacked the approval of a certified engineer. I was blown away. He insisted that the bikes would conflict with pedestrians at the intersections, even though the alternative he and our team had put forth instead placed them in conflict with 4,000-pound metal vehicles. We certified the project ourselves and moved forward.

Mayor Adrian Fenty shaking hands with Minnesota congressman Jim Oberstar at the opening of the Pennsylvania Avenue bike lanes (Kurt Raschke, Flickr)

The Pennsylvania Avenue bike lanes opened to great fanfare in June 2010. Representative Blumenauer, U.S. DOT Secretary Ray LaHood, House Transportation Chair Jim Oberstar, Ward 2 council member Jack Evans, and my boss, Mayor Adrian Fenty, all came out with their bikes, rode it, and beamed during the ribbon cutting. Equally important, the team members and consultants that had made design mistakes, then corrections, and re-implemented the project in record time, also celebrated its success.

The completed Pennsylvania Avenue bike lanes (Elvert Barnes, Flickr)

Kids enjoying the Pennsylvania Avenue bike lanes (Elvert Barnes)

In the end, the mayor called me out on my mistakes, and then gave me the opportunity to fix them. As a result, we had one of the best ribbon cuttings of our tenure. I learned a lot of lessons from Adrian Fenty about having your team's back, letting them screw up, getting back on track, and celebrating their ultimate successes. My own failure and redemption on the Pennsylvania Avenue bike lanes project perfectly reflected my inherent support for risk taking that I needed to inspire in DDOT staff.

You need to push boundaries and undermine the status quo, or your work reverts to the codes, regulations, and standards that have become the caricature of bureaucracies. What's worse is that these standards often fail us, as they did in this instance, because they fail to encapsulate the dynamism of the city, the potential for engineers to creatively solve new problems, and the capacity of our citizens to see and embrace change. Today, Pennsylvania Avenue is a complete street with bike lanes, as it was once a street with streetcars, and may once have been a street with a tree-lined median (but never was). DDOT staff is still improving the project to this day and, after much prodding by the public, including yours truly, recently installed physical separation along almost the entire corridor. Years from now, another transportation director may change this street, the symbolic heart of American politics, yet again. I should hope so, for this will prove that our society continues to slough off its old skin and old habits in favor of new ones.

The ability to be open-minded and try new things often comes down to personality profiles. Mayor Fenty and I demanded that we change the way we did business in Washington and DDOT even when members of my own team dissented. Because the public was also demanding change and we were servants of the public, we persevered, and my tenure oversaw positive transformation on the ground.

Notes

1   Rory Carroll, "Silicon Valley's culture of failure… and 'the walking dead' it leaves behind," *The Guardian,* June 28, 2014; http://www.theguardian.com/technology/2014/jun/28/silicon-valley-startup-failure-culture-success-myth

Pennsylvania Ave Bike Lane

The Making of America's Complete Main Street

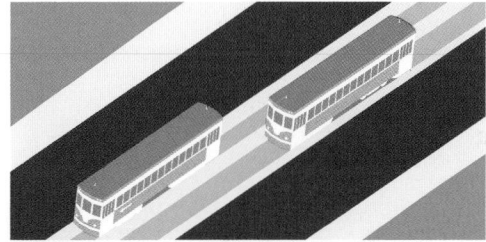

Until the 1960s, trolleys ran down the center of Pennsylvania Avenue, running past the White House to the Capitol.

The initial installation of the Pennsylvania Avenue bike lanes forwent the planned center-running design for a "safer" removal of two traffic lanes.

The story of the Pennsylvania Avenue bike lane (Infographic by Kate Chanba and David Vega-Barachowitz)

Untenable for many reasons, most significant being safety of cyclists dodging confused cars, the project was redesigned to the original plan, on the street, in record time.

Lesson #2

Manage S.M.A.R.T.

On managing others, empowering your team, and shamelessly promoting their accomplishments

I n my twenties, when I was a manager at Bikes USA, one of the nation's largest bike retailers, I had a great mentor named Casey Willson. Casey was vice president for human resources and, by all accounts, he was a fascinating character. He had an MBA and had worked in the Republican Party while teaching business classes in the early 1980s. But he was also a daily tai chi practitioner who had lived in Asia and rode his bike everyday to our offices in Alexandria from his condo in Washington, D.C.

Casey took me under his wing because he knew I was a "young buck," in his words, working seven days a week. He told me stories of importing funky Kalso Earth Shoes to the United States in the 1970s and opening a chain of stores where it was fine to smoke pot and take your shirt off if it was hot in the stock room (male or female). He also helped build a successful clothing chain named Britches of Georgetown and had put in place much of its management structure and training.

Casey first showed me that you could be fun, laid-back, and creative while also being organized in your management style, rigorous in your routine, and

> # I had become so indoctrinated with management theory in school, and so trained on performance and "winning," that I was professionally out of balance while working seven days a week in my "boss" guise.

demanding of yourself and your team. Although this felt counterintuitive based on my instincts at the time, I needed this lesson as a young manager who had created a clear delineation between my formal work self and my informal (true) self outside of work. I had become so indoctrinated with management theory in school, and so trained on performance and "winning," that I was professionally out of balance while working seven days a week in my "boss" guise. Looking back to those days, I had forgotten that people worked with me, and worked for me. Casey taught me by his example that you couldn't be a different person at home and at work. It's tiring and complicated and largely symptomatic of a failure to realize one of life's simple but basic lessons: *You gotta be you.*

If you're not, you're likely to encounter one of the following shortcomings as a manager:

- Have a disingenuous personality and management style
- Be too demanding, but not clear or communicative enough about your expectations
- Have a hard time performance-managing employees[1]
- Not enjoy your work

Starting out as a store manager at Bikes USA, I set a basic goal of increasing business immediately by at least 50 percent by paying more attention to the customer and capturing a greater share of the business walking through our door. To do that, we had to have (1) what people wanted when they came in (so every bike rack was full rather than empty), (2) better merchandising of soft goods (so most goods were not in storage in the back), and (3) the best salespeople working at the busiest times. By combining these strategies with publicly celebrating our highest-performing salespeople, we accomplished my goal within one to two weeks. After hitting this milestone, we worked hard to reinvent aspects of the business so that these changes were baked into the day-to-day routine. Every store I ran in the Washington, D.C., region went from the bottom three performers in the company (out of 21) to the top three, and often to number one, regardless of the location. As a result I was promoted to run all of the stores company-wide. I have learned that the same simple

Feeling valued is the most basic and most important motivator in any organization, and it is one of the things that I've most often found missing in large bureaucracies in particular.

approaches and management techniques work in a billion-dollar agency as in a $1-million or $50-million business.

When I arrived at Zipcar a couple of years later, I applied what I had learned about the importance of these simple management techniques—clear expectations and a structure that provides two-way communication and collaborative goal setting. This approach not only made people more comfortable and productive, it freed people from spinning their wheels so they could create new ideas and initiatives.

At Bikes USA, Zipcar, and in the public sector, I learned to embrace several critical and relatively simple ideas about management that I want to share here. The following lessons and stories span topics from pothole filling to hiring for success, but are bound by the basic idea that good managers have to be clear and definitive with their expectations, and can never forget that the people they are managing need to feel and be valued in order to take ownership of their work. Feeling valued is the most basic and most important motivator in any organization, and it is one of the things that I've most often found missing in large bureaucracies in particular.

1. *Embrace S.M.A.R.T. management and Six Sigma principles*[2]

Much of Zipcar's operational success and ability to scale was predicated on two integral approaches to management: S.M.A.R.T. and Lean Six Sigma. S.M.A.R.T. is a common mnemonic used in management that refers to the setting of clear, measurable objectives with your team. The mnemonic is based on the following principles—specific, measurable, agreed upon, realistic, time-sensitive—and this simple but hard-to-execute mantra was drilled into me by Casey Willson.

The S.M.A.R.T. approach to management (symbols adopted from TheNounProject.com; infographic by David Vega-Barachowitz)

The last, *time-sensitive,* is perhaps the most important on a day-to-day basis. I am continually amazed at how few goals set in organizations have a time stamp to measure whether the goal was met or not. How can you possibly know if you met your milestone on time without this? It is also very important when setting a goal with your team, or your boss, that you agree that it is feasible. If not, it is a goal that might be set by the boss with little or no buy-in from the employee, which can breed resentment once the goal is not met and performance management kicks in. Specific and measurable goals avoid ambiguity and confusion, because there are clear milestones to hit. When we were working on the many action agendas in D.C. and Chicago, we would sit in a room and test out goals for agreement. For example: "In-House Construction led by Tom will fill 20 percent more potholes (16,145) this season by May 1 by leveraging Potholepalooza [to be discussed later] for public participation, new hot asphalt, and contract teams during peaks." Or, "Jim and the bike team commit to complete 10 miles of new bike lanes this construction season (ending October 30) and 5 miles of restriping of old bike lanes, which hits our maintenance and new lane key performance indicators pledged to Mayor Fenty."

Lean Six Sigma, meanwhile, is a strategy for process improvement that originated in Japan and emerged from manufacturers like Motorola, Toyota, and GE in the 1970s and 1980s. It is a variability-reducing measure that dictates if you ever have to shut down the line in manufacturing, or you have a mistake that results in double work in an internal process, or you have a service error for a customer, you should STOP—it's a broken process. In America, we used to have, and often still do

S.M.A.R.T. and Six Sigma approaches to management can reduce the potential for confusion or duplicative work that results from misunderstandings.

have, an "acceptable error rate." Six Sigma says that anything less than 99.9999998 percent error rate, or 3.4 errors per million, is unacceptable. If there is an error, there must be a formal process to "lean out" the wasted steps in the process that led to the error. This process then ensures that error does not happen again.

Why is 99 percent not good enough? Let's use replacement tires for vehicles as an example. Michelin built their modern brand out of their brilliant slogan, "Because so much is riding on your tires," and we know that tires are genuinely a crucial safety mechanism for a vehicle. In 2013, 201.6 million replacement tires were sold. If 99 percent were error-free, that means more than 2 million defective tires would be shipped to consumers and installed, potentially affecting the safety of up to 2 million vehicles on the road. Is this acceptable? Absolutely not. But with Six Sigma, we end up with a maximum of just 686 faulty tires on the road. Our goal should be zero, but you get a sense of the ramifications in a high-volume, sensitive industry, and the effect. I believe that these same high standards should be applied to potholes, or to deaths on our roadways.

> Creatives, entrepreneurs, and planners often miss a big lesson here; they think that these kinds of strict processes eliminate creativity and eradicate flexibility. I would argue quite the opposite. Having a strong structural backbone in place frees people to be creative and take risks.

Embracing Six Sigma principles leads to a culture of continuous process improvement (CPI). CPI was a key to Zipcar's success in a capital-intensive business model as we scaled up. This stringent, yet highly collaborative, approach to constantly improving processes and creating the best products possible can be extended to service models as well, and even to how governments do business.

S.M.A.R.T. and Six Sigma approaches to management can reduce the potential for confusion or duplicative work that results from misunderstandings. They also provide a clear metric against which to measure regularly and performance manage. As a result, in your organizational culture, you can spend a lot less time "managing" day in and day out, which brings a more relaxed relationship with your team. You set goals with them, they work on these shared goals in a highly polished, process-oriented framework, and you have regular check-ins during which you help them figure out how to meet their milestones as opposed to harping on them that they need to work harder. Creatives, entrepreneurs, and planners often miss a big lesson here; they think that these kinds of strict processes eliminate creativity and eradicate flexibility. I would argue quite the opposite. Having a strong structural backbone in place frees people to be creative and take risks. When you test something, you are not just chasing your tail and experimenting, but intentionally trying something as part of a controlled experiment within a goal-oriented institutional framework.

When I went into the public sector, I adapted these same principles to bureaucracy and tried my best to ingrain these ideas within the culture of the agency as a whole. Local governments have a lot of multidisciplinary processes (imagine the life of a capital project from conception to construction). As a result, managers are often averse to addressing and fixing issues in which some part of the process is "out of their control." Moreover, governments have a lot of processes that are too bureaucratic, and often laden with twice as many handoffs as needed. What typically happens when the process is handed off from one person or department to another? Often, something is lost in the transfer—either clarity of purpose, an instruction, or possibly accountability for the task. In both D.C. and Chicago, a lot of what I did consisted of dissecting and then simplifying these processes to eliminate unnecessary handoffs between people and teams as much as possible, to force ownership and rebuilding of tasks and the associated processes. We ultimately reduced errors and oversights while increasing ultimate accountability for the finished product to one person or group.

In Washington, D.C., the entire senior management team was given Six Sigma training, and most of the team achieved white-belt status or higher (certification requires belt attainment, as in martial arts).

In Chicago, for instance, the agency's pothole program was in disarray when I arrived. As a result of a decade-old scandal surrounding asphalt deliveries being rerouted to private sites for profit, the program was wracked by paranoia, which caused a series of gross inefficiencies. Our crews, consisting of 200-plus workers, would go to the asphalt plant each morning at 8 A.M., wait for the asphalt to be loaded, patch potholes for two to three hours, take lunch, and then repeat before quitting halfway through the second load of asphalt, which would often get dumped under a bridge over a road that inevitably had potholes. Even though the asphalt plant could deliver directly to crews on-site, thereby expediting the process, the paranoia lingering from the "hired truck" scandal in Chicago had created a massive inefficiency of time, labor, and productivity to make sure that particular scandal didn't repeat itself. Even worse, I discovered that our crews were now using a material called "cold patch" in the summer to avoid inefficiency on the second shift. Cold patch bonds to asphalt at extremely low temperatures. In the summer, however, this material lasts literally about two days, tops, before heating up and being pulled back out by the warm tires of vehicles passing overhead.

After going down to the in-house construction division one morning, and spending time with the foreman who actually oversees the work day to day, we performed a basic "kaizen,"[3] and dissected the whole process using Six Sigma,

Resolving Chicago's Pothole Paranoia

How Chicago Dramatically Increased the Efficiency of the Pothole Program

Due to a scandal several decades ago, Chicago's pothole program suffered from severe inefficiency.

The process that Chicago's asphalt crews took to filling potholes wasted time and money, and resulted in far less production than expected.

A.M. crews report to work, then all drive to the asphalt plant.

Wait for truck to be filled.

Fill potholes. Repeat.

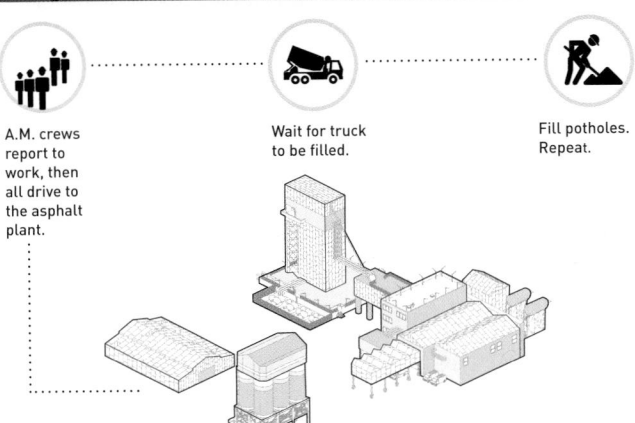

Due to a scandal a decade ago, a flawed system was designed primarily to avoid repeating the scandal vs. maximizing efficiency. This resulted in too many handoffs, lots of staff downtime, and out-of-season materials that didn't perform.

Utilizing continuous process-improvement strategy, a new process was redesigned with the foreman on the front lines and management, leaning out over half of the unnecessary steps, saving tens of thousands of dollars per week, and resulting in a higher volume of more-reliable patches in the streets.

Chicago pothole program explained (Symbols adapted from TheNounProject.com; infographic by Kate Chanba and David Vega-Barachowitz)

step by step, from when the crews clocked in through the end of the day. In this way, we first wanted to determine what the problem was, and then figure out a solution, likely by leaning out excess steps that were eating up potential efficiency. In the end, we figured out that the asphalt could be delivered on-site in the morning, with a second delivery to central points throughout the city, resulting in the crews working an extra three to four hours per day filling potholes, and/or using materials that actually lasted longer than forty-eight hours. In my first year on the job, our pothole program saw a complete overhaul and, combined with an innovative marketing strategy borrowed from Washington, D.C., Potholepalooza, we made the case to the public that we were actively trying to improve the conditions on our streets while saving the taxpayers significant, unnecessary overhead (see chapter 4).

> **Even as you are putting together a broader framework of goals and objectives, you have to fill the potholes, stripe the streets, put in the ADA ramps . . . and not just as well as your predecessor, but with an eye toward building on their work and dramatically increasing efficiency.**

Under Lean Six Sigma philosophy, when something goes "wrong," everyone needs to stop and recognize the "opportunity" to fix it, together, as opposed to letting the problem become the responsibility of the next person down the line, or creating a culture of subpar work being accepted as the norm. It takes away finger-pointing because everyone takes responsibility and works together, regardless of rank, to find a solution across disciplines. In this scenario, filling 95 percent of the potholes is considered a failure. Having four percent of our streetlights malfunctioning on a given day also represents a massive failure. Everyone plays a role in analyzing the problem, looking for solutions, and ultimately, raising the bar by dissecting the process and eliminating wasteful steps. As workers, we naturally want to jump to the conclusion that we can't hit the 99.9 percent goal because we're under-resourced, but the Lean Six Sigma process teaches you that you don't know that until you break down every aspect of the procedure and rebuild it properly. Only then do you really know what resources you actually need—often surprisingly little.

In both D.C. and Chicago, I found that I had to very quickly demonstrate that I could handle the basics of management like nobody's business if I wanted the powers that be to trust me with $100-million projects, as it should be. Even as you are putting together a broader framework of goals and objectives, you have to fill the potholes, stripe the streets, put in the ADA ramps . . . and not just as well as your predecessor, but with an eye toward building on their work and dramatically increasing efficiency.

2. Set clear, measurable, and ambitious goals

Goal setting may not be the sexiest topic, but without setting aggressive and agreed-upon targets with your stakeholders, you'll never get twice as much done in half the time. Goals can be configured and communicated in fun, creative, and visual ways. In the private sector, firms typically have a mission statement, and then set quantitative financial goals for the following year along with a growth percentage and a qualitative strategic plan that outlines new product launches, general marketing strategies, and so forth. In most companies, the line of business is pretty specific, so the strategy is evident unless new products or businesses are being rolled out or a significant strategic shift is planned. Some missions are big and broad. For example, Amazon.com, Inc., the retailer of everything, has this mission statement: "To be Earth's most customer-centric company, where customers can find and discover anything they want to buy online, and endeavors to offer its customers the lowest possible prices." Pretty ambitious. But guess what? They are executing it as a result.

When I started working in government, I found that the generally accepted management expectations were for a very well-organized budget and, to some extent, key performance indicators (KPIs), but this felt wholly inadequate to me. Why? Because we had an annual budget of approximately $1 billion in each city between capital and operating accounts (usually a ratio of 4:1 or 5:1), a tremendous amount of money to spend without a more cohesive strategy beyond budget allocations and a few loose goals. Furthermore, the breadth of our operation was such that we did everything from plow snow to fill potholes to build bridges and capitalize and launch transit services. Lastly, it seemed far too easy to fall into a pattern of focusing on one year at a time, which wouldn't give any manager enough runway to execute major initiatives. This short-term, siloed approach is one big reason for not getting things done in government. Agencies have often simply not laid out the big goals, how to accomplish them, and who does what beyond the big capital projects such as roads and bridges. Furthermore, they need to take these goals and break them down into manageable, achievable, and time-based chunks.

Our goal setting in D.C. took the form of an "action agenda," modeled on what Janette Sadik-Khan had spearheaded in New York City a couple of years earlier. In D.C., we started by talking to a lot of the advocates and activists in the community who cared about public space, transportation, and land use. We also consulted the business community, planners from other cities, architects, designers, progressive engineers, and our own internal teams over those first eight months. The result was our first action agenda, put out in 2009, which had more than 150 goals to hit in 24 months. Why 24 months? The mayor had two years left in his term should he not win re-election. Also, the action agenda was realistic, and the teams had all signed off; most of the initiatives could be completed in that time frame if we were hyperorganized and aggressive.

The reaction to the action agenda was uniformly positive, both internally and externally. Most importantly, the team at DDOT had a clear vision for the agency, a new mission and vision statement, and a renewed day-to-day focus with clearly defined, measurable, agreed-upon, realistic, and time-based objectives. This allowed us to spend the next year executing the agenda. We then reported on our progress and shortfalls, and set new goals within one year, with the action agenda update in 2010.

In Chicago, by contrast, I had already laid out more than one hundred goals when I took the helm at CDOT. The mayor had publicly proclaimed that we would put in one hundred miles of protected bike lanes, and that we would build the Bloomingdale Trail, a multi-use linear park retrofit along an unused, elevated rail line. Neither of these projects had any funding or a detailed plan behind it. Still, I put more than one hundred goals and metrics in front of him during our first meeting two weeks into his term, and he listened intently.

At the end of my initial presentation to him, Mayor Emanuel said, "Gabe, jeez, I thought you would come in with 2 to 3 goals for the first term; how can we possibly accomplish all of this?" It was a very reasonable question, and I knew that he was meeting with other cabinet members and doing some comparing and contrasting. I responded, "Mayor, if we set 2 to 3 goals, then we will come back in a couple of years and have achieved 1 to 2 of them, based on the odds. If we set 120 goals, and we achieve 70 to 90 of them, we will come back and feel accomplished, and you will be happy with me." He looked at me with a smirk-meets-a-smile, and said, "Okay, Gabe, whatever you think," which translated to, "You are the one who has to do all of this, so let's see what you've got."

3. *Measure your success (or failure)*

At DDOT we assembled a small group charged with documenting and verifying our performance across the agency on an ongoing basis against our stated goals. They would regularly report in our executive staff meetings where we were on track and where we were falling behind. Based on the goals we had accomplished in our first year, we often felt that we needed to set more aggressive targets for the following two years. This level of organization allowed us to surprise the public and release another updated action agenda for year two instead of waiting until the end of the twenty-four-month period, thereby updating our milestones and accomplishing more in a timely manner.

Nothing creates accountability better than tracking progress. Although the public certainly appreciates open data, we wanted to go one step further and manipulate the data so that the average consumer could understand the big trends more easily.

This collective benchmarking and goal-setting process had an added benefit. When Mayor Fenty lost the election in a hyperpolitical battle, and during the equally political transition, our amazing executive team worked with the performance management group to quickly assemble a more than 700-page transition report documenting all of our accomplishments. We put together the entire report in 72 hours because we had already done the hard work to build the vision and framework all the way down to the individual key performance indicators and tracked our progress every step of the way. We even built a data portal for getting public feedback and tracking performance in bus service, bike share, and all other large-scale capital projects.[4] Our goal was to make the agency transparent and accountable to the public, while also creating a new graphical user interface for interactivity. An added benefit of the project portal was comprehensive data collection and organization, so that when the powers that be wanted to criticize us for political reasons, the press backed us up and could refer to all of our transparent data sources.

Nothing creates accountability better than tracking progress. Although the public certainly appreciates open data, we wanted to go one step further and manipulate the data so that the average consumer could understand the big trends more easily. Are capital projects in your neighborhood being delivered on time? On budget? Are buses and bike share performing as promised? How about letting the public rate the quality of your services? All of this and more was publicly available and created a constant feedback loop for managers and staff running these programs and projects.

4. *Hire for the trait as opposed to the skill*

When I took the helm at DDOT, Mayor Fenty gave me free rein to hire, fire, and promote people as I saw fit. He was keen on empowerment and not second-guessing the people he had appointed to leadership posts. Hiring a strong team is incredibly difficult, and I could never have accomplished all I did without the aid and loyalty of my key deputies and advisors, some of whom were with me in both D.C. and Chicago.

I have hired many people in my career thus far. After a while, you learn to trust your instincts. Certain positions require a particular educational focus or achievement, such as chief engineer or general counsel. Others do not, such as public information officer, chief of staff, director, commissioner—or CEO, for that matter!

My biggest piece of advice for new managers is to hire for the trait as opposed to the skill. This means that you should not be wowed by what's on paper and disregard what's in front of you. I have hired people with no educational or professional background in a given area who have turned out to be exceptional performers because they have a wonderful and positive personality, intellect, and drive. I have also hired people based on their impressive credentials who have turned out not to be a good fit. This is uniformly because I chose to ignore the lack of traits that breed success in working with me. I am not saying that everyone you hire needs to be effusive, bubbly, and fun. That's not realistic. Some folks are quiet, Type B, high performers, but you want people who are dynamic in their own way, have a can-do attitude, and believe that where there's a will, there's a way. The only thing limiting our success is the limitations that we put on ourselves.

Diversity is a critical element in any workplace and needs to be reflected in how and whom you hire. I have been most successful when I have had a diverse team, and I always ensure that I do. I hire the best fit for the job, to work with me, and to round out the team to get things done. And when I hire the best, with no bias, I have women, people of color, young, and old in management ranks. Too much male energy can be counterproductive. Too many people from the same walk of life can be problematic. For instance, if all of your engineers are white males from the suburbs and you are serving a diverse population of men and women in the city, there are bound to be problems.

In my mind, a key component of continuous process improvement is a constant feedback loop, and this applies not only to things or services, it applies to people and their performance.

5. Give consistent, constructive feedback

In my mind, a key component of continuous process improvement is a constant feedback loop, and this applies not only to things or services; it applies to people and their performance. You should always be giving feedback to your team and making sure that they are, in turn, giving feedback to their team members. Ideally, this should take the form of structured and unstructured communication, including regular, ideally twice-yearly, review sessions that measure success against previous goals and set new goals in a collaborative fashion. Between these structured sessions, regular casual feedback is crucial; letting employees know that you recognize their good work goes a long way toward feeling appreciated. Letting employees know when they are falling short and giving them feedback on what they might change to be successful is equally important.

More broadly, for the past fifteen years, and because it was required of me at Zipcar, I have always had a formal mechanism for ensuring weekly feedback to me from my executive team in the form of a blog. With every position I hold, the communication gets a little bit better. In Chicago, I was really proud that as DOT commissioner, my weekly required blog filtered down to the managers on the front lines via their managers, and this happened organically. As a result, I received weekly feedback from everyone from the electrical operations manager and the asphalt foreman all the way up to the executive team at my level. This feedback proved extremely valuable. Because my boss,

> ## If you embrace these simple management techniques, you are more likely to have a staff that feels consistently guided, empowered, appreciated, and trusted.

Rahm Emanuel, would then actually respond weekly to my blog, I also started to write feedback on every blog and go over it in a weekly staff meeting with the senior leadership team, rather than just reading their posts, as I had previously. You never want to stop improving your communication, and you never want to fall out of touch with the people on the front lines doing the hardest work. If you do, you will not be as respected by your team, and you will not be as successful in your work outcomes.

6.   Have fun

If you embrace these simple management techniques, you are more likely to have a staff that feels consistently guided, empowered, appreciated, and trusted. You are also more likely to feel good about your own position, and this will free you up to be yourself at work. You can actually be "friends" with people that work for you if you put the effort into consistent performance management, which relieves the pressure of "subjective misunderstandings." Instituting this structure actually frees you up to be more creative, and to have fun rather than be stressed and inefficient.

I always tell my team and personally live by the maxim, "If it's not fun, don't do it!" I don't want to say that all work is going to be easy, or that you won't have horrible days when you ask yourself, "Why am I doing this?" There will always be ups and downs. I also believe in the old clichés "no pain, no gain," and "nothing worth doing is ever easy." But if the culture you have created for your organization and the work that you are doing is not inspiring your passion and fun, at least the majority of the time, then they are not working. My proudest moments have been when I've finished a job and gotten an outpouring of communication from employees telling me how much fun they had, and the effect that had on how much they accomplished during my tenure. For me, there is no greater professional satisfaction than this.

Notes

1 Performance management is a process by which managers and employees work together to plan, monitor, and review an employee's work objectives and overall contribution to the organization.

2 There are many resources on S.M.A.R.T. and Six Sigma management techniques, including *The Toyota Way: 14 Management Principles from the World's Greatest Manufacturer* by Jeffrey Liker (New York: McGraw-Hill), 2004. and *The One Minute Manager* by Kenneth H. Blanchard and Spencer Johnson (New York: William Morrow), 2003.

3 True Japanese business philosophy defines "kaizen" as the overarching system and philosophy for continuous process improvement. At Zipcar, we called the process of formal collaboration to break a process down and rebuild it "kaizen."

4 See the Ride DC portal dashboard at https://ridedc.ddot.dc.gov/

Lesson #3

(Kate Joyce Studios)

Where There's a Will, There's a Way

On how to evaluate your budget quickly, assess and align your stakeholders, and build beautiful cities (in no time)

T hus far, we have talked about the building blocks of good management, those challenges of working in cities, and how to begin to overcome the challenges. Now comes the most strategic bit: How do you come into a complex environment and set up the pins quickly to bowl a strike almost every time? To illustrate how to come into a new role, quickly assess your budget and stakeholders, and find opportunities where others saw red tape, I want to share the story of Chicago's Riverwalk.

Chicago's Riverwalk

When I took over the Chicago DOT on May 16, 2011, a few projects on my to-do list were marked HPP (high priority project). However, two weeks after I started, a project that was not on my original list of goals at all became a priority. Our deputy chief engineer, Dan Burke, and the manager of our Chicago River initiatives, Michelle Woods, asked to have a meeting with me that had an aura of "hush hush." We met and they educated me about the history of the Chicago

Riverwalk: the two of ten blocks that had been renovated, the dilapidated state of the other eight, and the as yet unrealized potential for its future.

In Washington, D.C., DDOT had worked extensively along the Anacostia River with our partner agencies to revitalize the Southeast and Southwest waterfronts, building a boathouse, the Anacostia Riverwalk Trail, pedestrian and bike bridges over the CSX railroad tracks, and the 11th Street bridges. So, we had an active role in D.C. But in Chicago, it was a big step up. I learned that with its

Construction of the Chicago Riverwalk (Shuja Kazi)

Chicago Riverwalk in bloom (Jeff Bowen)

rich history along the Chicago River and the lakefront, I had inherited a secondary title: "Harbor Master." My team said that in the historical code I was even required to always carry a special hat and a bugle (which they subsequently presented to me).[1]

Ten years prior, CDOT had constructed the first two blocks of a new riverwalk. This initial redesign actually served as a war memorial and provided a great basis for the project, but was very sterile and distinctly lacking in what my expectation would be for public life, recreation, or even business activity. Dan and Michelle envisioned a world-class riverwalk that could rival San Antonio's or Vancouver's—a gleaming example of industrial re-use along the riverfront.

At the end of the meeting, they had an ask. Would I move $1 million from another project to fund a conceptual design for the eight remaining blocks along the Chicago River? They had already lined up the finest national and local architects and designers under the prior administration, including Sasaki Associates out of Boston and Carol Ross Barney in Chicago. Without hesitation, I agreed. "Let's do it." As soon as I saw the project, the quality of their presentation, and their passion for it, I knew that somehow we would figure out the project funding to build it in a short time frame and keep it from being stalled for the next ten years. It was too good an opportunity to ignore, and I appreciated their devotion to the project.

When I had met with the mayor a week earlier to discuss my goals, the riverwalk wasn't one of the projects that I had pitched him on, because I had not known about it myself. After seeing it, I knew that this was something Mayor Emanuel would like, but until we had a compelling design, and a politically viable way to pay for it, I would keep the project under wraps. How could I keep a large project expenditure under wraps? This is why you need to get to know, and exploit, every flexibility in your budget to get sh*t done. Often, money in one project can be flexed to another project without administrative or legislative approval if the amount is below a threshold. Federal funds can be moved via the Transportation Improvement Program at the regional metropolitan planning organization. A third option is to flex an expenditure within a project that also serves a larger purpose—for example, purchasing a new software package for agency-wide capital budgeting within a large, complex project that also

The problem was, it was the day before our meeting, and not only had I not prepared a finely tuned presentation for Secretary LaHood and his senior team, I had not even told the mayor about it because the people around him hadn't wanted me to show him the project.

needs that functionality. Leah Treat, our deputy director for finance in D.C. and managing deputy for administration and finance in Chicago, had actually done this at DDOT with the 11th Street bridges. She put a capital planning tool into the $365 million budget for the project that directly benefited and saved money on the bridges, but also resulted in an ongoing capital planning tool being put in place for the whole agency. A fourth flexibility is to use the metropolitan planning organization or federal contracting tools such as the GSA schedule, which can allow an agency to co-opt contracts regionally, and sometimes nationally, to replicate success in another jurisdiction without going through a lengthy procurement.

As a result of our creativity, one year later, we had a beautiful design document that our team of contractors had put together. I say "team of contractors"

Rendering of Chicago Riverwalk showing the theater (Ross Barney Architects, Sasaki Associates, Jacobs/Ryan Associates, Alfred Benesch & Company)

Rendering of Chicago Riverwalk showing State and Dearborn (Ross Barney Architects, Sasaki Associates, Jacobs/Ryan Associates, Alfred Benesch & Company)

purposely, because I am a big believer in the integration of contractors with your team. In an ideal world, these contractors become an extension of your internal team and that alignment plays out in the quality of the end product. The design that Sasaki, Carol Ross Barney, and their partners came up with created a series of unique public "rooms" with a different theme for each block. It was beautiful. We were ready to bring the project to the mayor.

I tried and tried to get in to see the mayor after showing the design to his office and the city budget office, but to no avail. The budget situation was so dire due to years of borrowing, not making tough choices, rich labor agreements, and entitlements coming due that the powers that be did not want me to show the mayor a shiny new project with a $100 million price tag. And based on the broader financial situation, I understood their fear. However, I learned in the business world that when things are tough, that's when you have to get creative, and often double down risk-wise to be successful. In this case, if we pulled it off, the return on investment would be tremendous, and the benefits to the city and citizens were undeniable. Our team was prepared to put forth a full financial plan to pay for the project without further stressing the fragile budget, and I knew we could pull it off.

Three months later, Mayor Emanuel, the heads of the Chicago Transit Authority, Chicago Aviation, and I were in Washington, D.C., to meet with U.S. Secretary of Transportation Ray LaHood for our yearly update on the state of our transportation system. This was also the time to outline our big programs for the U.S. DOT leadership team, as well as our asks for what we thought we could finagle that year financially and administratively based on the current state of affairs in Washington. The largest U.S. cities keep lobbying operations in Washington, D.C., and our director of legislative affairs, Melissa Green, had seen our project and really liked it. The problem was, it was the day before our meeting, and not only had I not prepared a finely tuned presentation for Secretary LaHood and his senior team, I had not even told the mayor about it because the people around him hadn't wanted me to show him the project. Now I had to scramble.

The night before the big meeting at U.S. DOT, the mayor met with all of us in the D.C. office of the City of Chicago on Pennsylvania Avenue. I looked out at the bike lanes that I had put in against all odds a few years before and said to myself, screw it, I know some people will be mad at me, but we didn't come all this way for nothing, and my team had not put in all of this work just to see their vision stalled again due to internal politics.

I was the last to present to Mayor Emanuel. I looked at Melissa. She nodded and mouthed, "Show it to him." So I pulled out the designs and walked the mayor through the project block by block. As I presented, I could feel his energy building as he got more and more excited. He said, "This is a legacy project," and I realized that he instantly understood the magnitude of the project and the effect it could have on Chicago's downtown public space and tourism efforts, while creating a citywide amenity for generations.

Then, I brought up our plan to fund it. Scott Kubly, one of my two managing deputies who had come with me from Washington, D.C., and one of the most creative transportation finance people in the country, had put together a plan

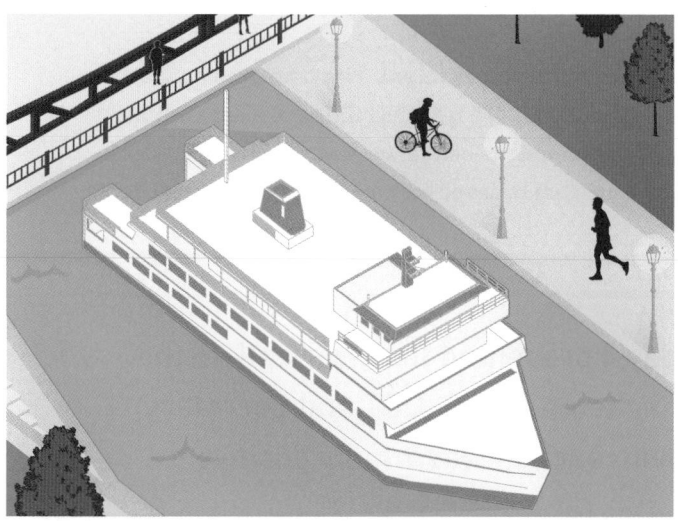

Riverwalk Revival, Fast

How Chicago Got Creative & Aligned Incentives to Fund the Riverwalk

Outside of two blocks that had been renovated in the mid 2000s, the Chicago Riverwalk was mostly dark, stagnant, inaccessible, and underutilized as a result. $1 beers were sold mere blocks from the "Magnificent Mile."

The two blocks of ten that had been renovated were a great anchor for the project and proved that a contiguous, expanded space was a vast improvement. However, the design was for a war memorial and the eight other blocks needed to be more people-oriented.

Sasaki, Carol Ross Barney, and a team of subcontractors put together a brilliant design with eight "rooms" focused on people.

The City pitched and was awarded a TIFIA loan with a 35-year payback in a record 8 months. The biggest beneficiaries of the new Riverwalk, the tour boats, paid increased fees for their new, enhanced home and long-term leases. This paid for the bulk of the project. Remaining income came from advertising, sponsorship, and rent from new retail spaces.

to rebid our tour boat fees to pay for the project. Leah Treat, our other managing deputy who had finance within her CDOT responsibilities, worked with Scott and me and stress tested the assumptions before we sent them to the chief financial officer (CFO). If my core team believed we could do it, I would back the project 100 percent.

The following day, I presented the riverwalk to the entire leadership team at U.S. DOT and Secretary LaHood. Their reaction was wholly positive.

If we qualified for a thirty-five-year federal Transportation Infrastructure Finance and Innovation Act (TIFIA) loan, we could pay back more than two-thirds of the loan with the increased fees from a rebidding of just two boat slips used for architecture tours.[2] The slips had been cash cows for many years but were well below market rate. By aligning public and private incentives, the architecture tour companies would pay a fair amount more, but would get a greatly enhanced riverwalk to operate from, which would grow their business. Additionally, by giving them longer-term agreements, the tour operators would gain the security they need to recapitalize their fleets and make business plans for expansion. Additional revenues would come from retail space created along the new riverwalk, meters for private boats, and advertising and sponsorship of blocks. Mayor Emanuel said, "I love it! Why didn't you bring this to me sooner?"

The following day, I presented the riverwalk to the entire leadership team at U.S. DOT and Secretary LaHood. Their reaction was wholly positive. As it turns out, they were tired of getting repetitive TIFIA loan submissions for highway tolling projects, and they saw this as an opportunity to exhibit a completely different type of project—one that could showcase maritime and active river transportation, dramatic pedestrian and accessibility improvements, sustainability, and public space innovation—using the newly expanded (with bipartisan support) TIFIA loan program.

With a green light from the mayor's office and U.S. DOT, over the next eight months, our team worked on the financial pro forma, plan, project engineering, and outreach. With incredible support and work from Chicago's CFO, Lois Scott, and her crackerjack finance team, we closed on the fastest TIFIA loan in U.S. DOT history—a mere eight months (the fastest prior had been eighteen months). The unprecedented partnership amongst stakeholders trumped all of the naysayers who had said that the project was too expensive, that we couldn't take on the risk, and it was too much, too fast.

But that's not all. At the time, CDOT was already working on the Wells Street Bridge project on the Chicago River. This was an incredibly complex, multilevel bascule bridge with maritime traffic underneath, bicycle, pedestrian, automobile, and bus traffic on the first level, and the Chicago Transit Authority operating trains on the second level. The firm that was performing the work on the bridge,

Walsh Construction, a national firm based in Chicago, also bid and won the riverwalk project. As they put the finishing touches on the bridge in October 2013, they moved their staging equipment right over to the riverwalk and began that project the following month. We aimed to build phase one, the first four blocks of the riverwalk, within four years of conceiving of the project, and within the mayor's first term, rather than the average of thirteen years. The first phase opened in May 2015.

The fact that we moved a megaproject from conception to design to public outreach, then funding, engineering, and construction in twenty-eight months, as opposed to the typical seven to nine years for project development, may

Chicago Riverwalk (Michael Shall)

be surprising to some, but it can be done. Projects of the scale of the Chicago Riverwalk are not uncommon in large American cities. These sites are studied, planned for, designed, and often even engineered, but in many cases, then not implemented for years, if at all. Politics, changes in administrations and priorities, and funding shortfalls can all derail the best of intentions, and the passage of time is the worst foe for ambitious projects.

There are many lessons here, but I want to emphasize a few key points:

- "Make no little plans," as architect and urban planner Daniel Burnham once said. The project, and its presentation, had to be grand and ambitious enough to grab Mayor Emanuel's interest and commitment, as well as that of the public and U.S. DOT.
- Get creative financially. A financial plan was developed that paid for the project by aligning the incentives of the private sector with those of the public sector. The biggest beneficiaries of the project, the tour boat industry, did not mind paying more for a project that was going to enhance their business. Moreover, we didn't let the initial lack of funding scare us from pursuing the project because there were many potential revenue streams.
- Don't let doubt and frustration stymie good projects. In spite of their best efforts, we did not allow the naysayers to deter us from doggedly pursuing the funding and approvals for the project.

The Dearborn bike lane: The "game changer"

Although the Chicago Riverwalk represents one of the best examples of how to overcome opposition and persevere in the face of doubt, these ideas also apply to projects that are smaller in scale, if not in their overall significance. In 2013, PeopleForBikes (formerly known as Bikes Belong), a national advocacy organization and foundation that supports bicycling, named the Dearborn bike lane in Downtown Chicago the best bike lane in America.[3] A bidirectional facility with dedicated bicycle signals, Dearborn changed how many in Chicago felt about commuting by bike to their jobs in the Downtown Loop and served as a catalyst for the further expansion of the city's bike network. Due to its central location and the density of stakeholders in the area, the lane should have been a major challenge to get on the ground. Yet looking back, the preparation and outreach by CDOT and our partners made what should have been a tough sell into an easy one. We assessed and aligned our stakeholders, brought together our staff around a common, implementable vision, and made the project work within a year, on the cheap.

During my first eight months, our outreach for the Chicago Streets for Cycling Plan 2020 and the resulting feedback made it clear to us that Chicagoans were eager to have safer bike facilities near their homes, but also desired citywide connectivity, particularly to and through the Loop, if they were going to consider commuting by bike. Like most of our key projects, we had assembled a big tent of supporters to make sure that we had maximum reach, input, and backing when we went public with the 2020 bike plan. The plan as process and output proved a critical first step because of the potential for blowback from

Dearborn bike lane (Gabe Klein)

auto-oriented skeptics, many of whom still viewed bikes as nothing more than a recreational activity for kids or a form of high-intensity fitness training.

In the plan, we could not and did not ignore the complexities of downtown traffic, which previous plans had skirted due to its heavy congestion and high stakes. The Dearborn two-way bike lane represented the centerpiece of the proposal for the Chicago Loop and was, in many ways, the route without which the entire thing would fall apart. In other words, to paraphrase Mayor Emanuel, we better not mess this one up. Quite a bit of traffic engineering was necessary to ensure that we could make everyone, including kids and grandparents, feel safe along the route. We even tried to find intersections where we could improve the signal timing for vehicular throughput, because many of the intersections had

> **Aim high, don't shy: We took on the center of the downtown to solve a real problem, rather than working peripherally because "it was too hard."**

not been significantly changed since the 1970s, yet traffic patterns and mode choice had changed considerably since then. Our planners and engineers had ventured to put a two-way bike lane on an otherwise one-way street, a rare feat in the Midwest (at the time), so fine-tuning the turning movements and signal operations became absolutely essential. Early on, our engineers made the decision to add turn lanes for cars and signalize them with dedicated arrows and signal timing, along with additional dedicated signals for bicycles, a relatively new approach in the United States, putting Chicago at the forefront of the bicycle renaissance from Portland to New York. After months and months of planning, the CDOT team was ready to go.

Toward the middle of the design phase, we called on the Active Transportation Alliance, a fifty-person advocacy organization fighting for the needs and rights of pedestrians, cyclists, and transit users in Chicagoland since the 1980s. They worked seamlessly with our admittedly sparse team to knock on every single business's door along the entire corridor of more than a mile to explain the project, how it would affect them, and why it was going to be good for commerce. A few businesses still had concerns after meeting with our bike team and the Active Transportation Alliance, so I met with them personally, which ultimately saved considerable time. With a few tweaks and some convincing, we were able to get near 100-percent buy-in from the business community.

Internally, we built support for the project by challenging our engineers to strive for greatness and to use the latest technology, including sensors to detect cars in the turn lanes and cyclists approaching the lights to trigger a light change. Our Bureau of Electricity, our line striping unit, and CDOT inspectors were employed to implement the project as opposed to contractors. So, at every level of the agency, CDOT staff had a role in this high-profile, high-stakes project, and everyone was aligned to see it succeed. We also had total control and were able to use CDOT internal budget line items for the bootstrap project. We had no dedicated funding stream for bike lanes for the first two years—just a mandate—so creativity was key.

Outreach is essential: We leveraged the enthusiasm and skill of our partners, in particular the Active Transportation Alliance, to do robust outreach to the business community and the public for this and other projects such as bus rapid transit.

At the eleventh hour, we learned that the Illinois DOT, which had jurisdiction over a few of the east-west streets that crossed the Dearborn bike lane, was going to flex its political muscle. A year before, we had planned on running a protected bike lane from the west side of Chicago all the way through the Loop, and the state traffic engineers had balked because "they had jurisdiction" and "this was unproven." This was really code for "we are not going to let you do it . . . just because." These sorts of jurisdictional battles are a common thread in cities where historical ownership of certain streets, particularly larger arterials, by the state can result in shockingly simple ideas being portrayed as radical. What I didn't count on was Illinois DOT banning us from even crossing one of their streets or adding one bicycle signal. However, there were bigger political and personality issues and tensions at hand between the city and state. The governor's office didn't want me or the city dictating policy to them, or making the state look "old school in the face of change." The Illinois DOT, because of many overtures at the engineers' level, was actually on board with our bike and safety projects at this point and supported our overall approach.

Keep in mind that we were literally getting ready to stripe the streets at this stage of the game. The striping had been planned for two consecutive weekends so as to not disturb rush hour traffic on weekdays. Our goal was to have people leave on Friday at 5 P.M. and return Monday to a new street. We wanted to get in and get out, with no time for people to get riled up over construction or an un-used, empty facility—another big lesson for transportation agencies in avoiding unnecessary flack.

In many cities, this political obstinacy from the governor's office would have stalled, if not killed the project, but we refused to give in to this totally unreasonable prohibition. As we looked for a way out we realized that we had been maintaining and adjusting the signals at the intersections for decades, and so, based on precedent, the state had forfeited the right to dictate individual planning decisions at the intersection level. Our engineers also determined that we could suspend the markings at the state intersection if we were ultimately forced to without any significant compromise to safety. If people asked why we had done this, we would tell them.

Bike signals were a relatively new feature when they were used on the Dearborn bike lane (Bike Walk Lincoln Park)

We sent a note to our friends at the state, knowing that they were ruffling our feathers at the behest of the governor's office for political reasons, rather than disagreeing with the decision based on any sound engineering or planning basis. We notified them respectfully that we were charging ahead with the project, the reasons why we were justified, and that they were invited to the press event to unveil the project if they so chose. We came from a strong position, and did not back down. Basically, we were saying, "Go ahead and sue us."

The state, as I predicted, stayed quiet as the facility went in. As the bike lane became real, and people started riding in it before it was even open, we heard no complaints, save one hotel that needed some adjustments made to a loading zone. No complaints!? I thought to myself, is my team hiding the nasty e-mails from me? No, nothing. How could this be? Here are some keys to success:

- Initial feedback and data collection showed that vehicular operations were unchanged or actually improved with the dedicated turning facilities and signals.
- Pedestrians liked the shorter crossing distance, and the cyclists went from 31 percent abiding by signals to 81 percent immediately, with fewer conflicts overall.
- The project was aesthetically pleasing, and used green paint at conflict areas. Combined with the new signalization, the street felt more organized and safer overall.

- The Active Transportation Alliance and the CDOT bike team did a superb job getting input from affected businesses and building owners, quelling concerns and making adjustments where needed.
- The project became a team-building exercise for everyone, from myself to the deputies of every division, to the front line striping units and electrical workers.
- The Dearborn bike lane had its own Twitter account. Ok, I am kidding that this was a key to success, but seriously, someone started @dearbornbikeln during the week it launched (and it's still active). The mayor's office even recognized its existence in a tweet. People loved it.

Dearborn bike lane (National Association of City Transportation Officials)

We had a press conference, and more than two hundred Chicagoans showed up to celebrate the new facility. It was a landmark project for Chicago, and it made a statement that we were serious about safety, as well as about cycling as

Build internal support and capacity: We built internal support at every level of CDOT by giving everyone a role to play.

a form of basic urban transportation. At the launch ceremony, the mayor challenged other cities to up the ante and said that Chicago was aiming to take jobs from Portland and Seattle by offering a better quality of life for our citizens. Mayor McGinn of Seattle responded in kind a few days later saying, "Rahm Emanuel wants our bikers and tech jobs. We are going to work to keep them right here."

Our team, blue collar and white collar, came out in force and shared in the pride of the successful project. Even former Olympic cyclist John Vande Velde and his son, professional cyclist Christian Vande Velde, both Chicagoans, came out for the inaugural ride. We had pulled off the unthinkable, in record time, with no vocal opposition, in the densest area of the city.

As the PeopleForBikes article stated, "Chicago's 1.2-mile showpiece isn't the country's most sophisticated downtown bikeway because of its on-street markings, though they're excellent, or its quick-and-simple plastic-post barriers. The really remarkable thing about Dearborn is that bikes get their own traffic signals. Maybe that's why stoplight compliance has soared from 31 percent to 81 percent and bike traffic has more than doubled since the lane went in. Did we mention that one of its local fans has given the lane its own Twitter feed? We challenge any other street project in the country to inspire such devotion."[4]

What should you do?

- **Aim high, don't shy:** We took on the center of the downtown to solve a real problem, rather than working peripherally because "it was too hard."
- **Outreach is essential:** We leveraged the enthusiasm and skill of our partners, in particular the Active Transportation Alliance, to do robust outreach to the business community and the public for this and other projects such as bus rapid transit.
- **Don't let the politics scare you into submission:** We didn't let the state government defeat a strong project on political grounds. We moved forward regardless and used our detailed knowledge of the site as a lever to get what we wanted.
- **Build internal support and capacity:** We built internal support at every level of CDOT by giving everyone a role to play.

(Kate Joyce Studios)

Mayor Rahm Emanuel at the podium for the Dearborn bike lane launch

Notes

1. From *The Municipal Code of Chicago: Comprising the Laws of Illinois Relating to the City of Chicago, and the Ordinances of the City Council,* by Barnard Beach, 1881, page 324, number 1322, "The Harbor Master shall at all times while on duty carry a speaking trumpet, which shall be his badge of office, and through which his orders can be heard at a distance."

2. "The Transportation Infrastructure Finance and Innovation Act (TIFIA) program provides Federal credit assistance in the form of direct loans, loan guarantees, and standby lines of credit to finance surface transportation projects of national and regional significance. TIFIA credit assistance provides improved access to capital markets, flexible repayment terms, and potentially more favorable interest rates than can be found in private capital markets for similar instruments. TIFIA can help advance qualified, large-scale projects that otherwise might be delayed or deferred because of size, complexity, or uncertainty over the timing of revenues. Many surface transportation projects—highway, transit, railroad, intermodal freight, and port access—are eligible for assistance. Each dollar of Federal funds can provide up to $10 in TIFIA credit assistance—and leverage $30 in transportation infrastructure investment." Federal Highway Administration, http://www.transportation.gov/tifia

3. Anderson, M., "America's 10 Best Protected Bike Lanes of 2013," People for Bikes, December 03, 2013, http://www.peopleforbikes.org/blog/entry/the-10-best-protected-bike-lanes-of-2013. http://www.dnainfo.com/chicago/20131204/loop/dearborn-street-bike-lane-named-best-protected-route-of-2013

4. Ibid.

Lesson #4

(get directly down, Flickr)

Sell Your City

On marketing your projects, communicating with the public, and celebrating your accomplishments

As a kid and then as a young adult working in my dad's retail bicycle stores, I was obsessed with the front window displays. Every week, I went out of my way to reorganize the layout of our stores to ensure that regular customers were greeted with novel product lines and new merchandise that we were ordering to keep the experience of visiting fresh. I started assembling group rides for enthusiasts and even sponsored a race team to deepen our ties to the weekend warriors who regularly patronized the shops. From a young age, I found a creative niche in business by linking great products and services with a sensitivity to our customers' lifestyle ideals and preferences.

I went on to study marketing and management in college and was excited to learn that marketing didn't equate to advertising alone. Advertising represented only one aspect of a more complex marketing environment that encompassed the product or service as well as the target market, the associated pricing, the channel of delivery, and the overall promotion strategy. I appreciated how marketing naturally grew out of and aligned with good management and strong communication. These ideals provided me with a foundation for undertaking new ideas in the private and public sectors and encouraged me to embrace the notion that regardless of your line of work, you are ultimately selling something, and that selling can be fun and provide a feedback loop that makes your offering better and better. Marketing is also essentially the core psychology of business. In business, you need to understand your customers' needs, likes, and dislikes, and then segment those characteristics to appeal to what they want and understand what will make them adopt something in the long term.

At both Bikes USA and Zipcar, standardized marketing was critical to our success. These companies needed to preserve their brand across stores and cities to maintain a strong and consistent reputation, even as individual locations and managers maintained their own unique character. Conformity was never the goal. Rather, we wanted to ensure that the "brand promise" meant something and was adhered to. This promise, in turn, was intrinsically bound to a vision and mission for the organization. These kinds of structures, and the consistent management that underlies them, actually allow for more creativity and experimentation rather than stifling individual expression. The consistent reinforcement of a company's mission and culture, and how that manifests itself in customer interactions, makes all the difference. It is these details that attract people to certain brands, and deter them from embracing others. Brands such as Virgin, Apple, and Chipotle are top-flight because of the value of their offering, which is tied to the quality standards they adhere to, consistently, for a fair price. I would also venture that they are extremely creative precisely as a result of this, not in spite of it. When you are on solid footing operationally, and know who you are and what you stand for as a brand, it allows you to focus externally on serving the customer rather than internally on process breakdowns and culture clashes.

In college, I had a marketing professor with whom I got into a public argument in class. She insisted that you could compete on quality or price, but not both. In the academic world of business, this was considered basic fact, but I took exception to that rule and still do. Services like Uber and Lyft, for instance, are genuinely outcompeting taxis on both fronts. The value they provide to the consumer consists of a better typical experience, a faster arrival time, and a lower cost (at least for now). By embracing technology, reducing friction in customer engagement, and attacking markets with stagnant or overregulated offerings, you can lower prices and improve quality and service, a trend that has been exhibited again and again in the sharing economy, peer-to-peer networks, and online retail.

Marketing your projects in the public sector

When I started at DDOT, I asked myself: Why should the private sector have a monopoly on high-quality marketing? On next-generation customer engagement? On technology-enabled products and services? I knew that our communications to stakeholders were generally fair to middling in quality and consistency, that we weren't very proactive, that we needed to listen more, and that some of our services had grown stale, if consistent.

One of the most important things I brought to the government beyond collective visioning, collaborative goal setting, and experience operating and delivering in business was the ability to communicate with the public effectively while empowering our great communications and public relations staff to open up the black box that had been instinctively created. Their first reaction was always shock. Really? We can talk about all of this stuff the agency does?

In D.C., people were not used to someone aggressively selling the program as much as I was, but the reaction was very positive internally within the government and externally with the business community and the public at large. The public appreciated our efforts and the ability to know our reasoning behind the projects we were undertaking, and there was a lot pride within the agency that we were being recognized. In fact, Karyn LeBlanc and John Lisle, who ran our communication and marketing efforts, were frequently asked to speak around the country about best practices in government communication. Our embrace of social media was one of the first in the country at that scale. From Twitter to Flickr to Scribd to our own blog and live chats with the public, the black box opened up and the public had the access they wanted and deserved.

In Chicago, meanwhile, there was far more confusion and skepticism within the government about our overhaul of the communications program. The culture of the political machine had taken a heavy toll on the city and its staff. The month before I arrived, Mayor Daley's commissioner of streets and sanitation was indicted. People casually joked that the next most likely position after someone was an alderman was cellmate.

Although I thought this was funny, it was also tragic, and dozens, if not hundreds, of Chicago and Illinois government workers had gone to jail over the past twenty years. To say the public lacked trust in the government is an understatement, and the honest people working in government were understandably shell-shocked from the constant scandal playing out in the papers and the courts.

Rahm Emanuel was coming in on the heels of twenty-two years of Mayor Richard M. Daley and forty-three years of Daley family control in total. Tumult, nervousness, and excitement ran amongst many government employees eager to turn to a new chapter, but many were also scared to find themselves on the cusp of a new era with unknown changes to come. Against this backdrop, in May 2011, I immediately adopted an open-door policy with the press and not only returned their calls without a great deal of oversight, but aggressively worked to sell the Emanuel administration's new vision for CDOT and beyond. The mayor and I articulated our goal of moving people within the context of creating jobs, healthier citizens, and a more robust economy—messages aligned with the mayor's mission. The public responded positively to it. Why? Because it was all true and was tied back to our stated goals. With few exceptions, we also received positive reaction from the rest of our key stakeholders, who had been long awaiting this change.

I had my battles with city hall to keep talking proactively to the press. The culture under Daley had been to avoid having your name in the paper if you could. We kept pushing, though, and rebranded the agency, rebooted our website, started social media accounts, and created a Complete Streets initiative—an effort to ensure that users of all modes of city transportation can travel safely and comfortably—over which we had full control. Meanwhile, I fired on all cylinders from my own Twitter account so that we could keep directly communicating with our constituents, and set a new standard for transparency and service.

Potholepalooza, communication, and participatory government

From my time in both Washington, D.C. and Chicago, my personal favorite example of creative marketing in the public sector was Potholepalooza. Our director of communications at DDOT, Karyn LeBlanc, was an outside-the-box thinker in government, but had not gotten the thumbs-up to exercise her talent. She needed a partner in crime to make sure her creative ideas hit the ground running. Wanting to empower and harness this energy, shortly after I started as director I asked her to work up some fun, unconventional concepts. She responded with a wealth of ideas, including one of my favorites, Potholepalooza.

Potholepalooza represented one of the agency's first attempts to make the mundane obligations of city government into something dynamic, relatable, and appreciated. As conceived, Potholepalooza aimed to accomplish a few key things:

- Involve the public in an interactive way, while transforming the reactionary function of government into something positive, fun, and actually proactive.

- Instill competition within the agency to perform publicly, transparently, and with minimal response time.
- Give the agency a new image, and not just in the bike or bus program, but also in the trenches for blue-collar workers doing the hard manual labor for our citizens.
- Take something with a negative connotation—potholes—and make them fun, recasting D.C.'s reputation as "pothole ridden."

Using our new Twitter page, "See-Click-Fix" (a new collaborative public reporting application), and good old-fashioned e-mail and phone, we launched Washington, D.C.'s first ever pothole-reporting blitz. After a press conference with Mayor Adrian Fenty and a slew of cameras, the reports (and often the associated images) came pouring in by the hundreds. We committed to fill reported potholes within forty-eight hours using thirteen crews on the streets. We also continued the use of vehicles called "pothole killers," which significantly automated the process and were a great high-tech complement to the standard pothole-filling crews.

It worked. During the three-month-long event, we filled six thousand potholes in record time. The public appreciated the quick response to their requests, and the team relished the collaboration with the public, the challenge, and the sense of camaraderie growing internally, not to mention all of the positive press. Potholepalooza had proven that a bad word—pothole—

could become a good word overnight, and that we didn't have to be scared of the public, social media, or the press.

When I got to Chicago (the actual home of the concert series Lollapalooza), a bigger city with a much harsher winter and associated pothole problem (and less money, to boot), we said screw it, let's replicate the campaign there.

I had to battle with our CDOT operations team to join me on this adventure because we were already stressed for resources. My attempt to bring pothole killers to Chicago had failed in what I perceived as sabotage by the unions, who were threatened by any type of automation. On top of that, Chicago had a prevailing culture of avoiding press and any challenge that could possibly result in failure. This was so firmly ingrained that people were reluctant to try anything new. We compromised and undertook a shortened version, with three days of reporting and seven days of pothole filling. Even so, in Chicago, the campaign garnered similar results and excitement as in D.C., and citizens felt like their government was involving them and proactively addressing their problems. They could also be part of the solution, and we made it fun. We filled 250,000 potholes before the event even began, and thousands more that week. The press release got national attention.

Opening the curtain

In Washington, D.C., the use of public data, competition, and apps went well beyond Potholepalooza. Under Mayor Fenty, chief technology officer Vivek Kundra, who eventually went on to become CTO for the federal government, started an open data effort for D.C. From potholes and streetlight outages to crime stats and purchasing information, all of our data became public. The city then held a crowdsourcing competition called Apps for Democracy to facilitate the public creation of applications based on these public data sets. It cost $50,000 in prize money and brought in forty-seven new applications worth an estimated $2.3 million. Both initiatives were hugely successful and set the tone for open data nationally and now internationally. By making everything public and more transparent, associated government performance metrics naturally started to improve.

It helped that we had an internal dashboard for every agency called "Track D.C." that allowed our teams to make sense of much of the data. This tracked overall spending versus budget, key initiatives completed, and customer service scores by the public.

It was in this very progressive climate that we set out to put a new face on the front of our transportation agency. These efforts resulted in a new social media program, the new DDOT Project Portal and Performance Dashboard, and the D.C. Circulator and Capital Bikeshare performance dashboards. The sum total of these efforts represented a complete makeover of the communications system, along with a new and consistent look, feel, and message. One of the biggest complaints I faced when coming into DDOT was that there was little proactive communication on most projects, and you had to e-mail and call multiple people for information, often resulting in inconsistent responses. Our agency rebranding communicated that we were open for, and competing for, your business and respect. The project dashboard took a tremendous amount of process work behind the scenes to get the engineers, planners, and management to use project management software rather than spreadsheets, and to upload updates to their projects every Friday for public consumption. We made as much data and project information as possible publicly available and created accountability both internally and externally to the citizens.

The Capital Bikeshare and Circulator Bus dashboards spearheaded by Scott Kubly and the tech team displayed a range of performance indicators. Unlike capital projects, these programs were operating entities that touched the public daily and incurred costs to the taxpayer if not run efficiently. Operating performance metrics were critical, but we also viewed customer ratings of these systems as key data points. The Circulator, which we oversaw in tandem with Metro, was operated by First Transit, a private entity. The Circulator service typically had close to a 98-percent customer service rating based on survey, well above the comparable Transit Authority–run local Metrobus service, which hovered around 80 percent. Like Potholepalooza, our marketing efforts entailed a complete reinvention of our services, with the ultimate goal of accountability to the public.

A marketing case study: Divvy bike share

Divvy bike share in Chicago provides another example of how to innovate in marketing a new transit option. Unlike D.C.'s Capital Bikeshare, in Chicago, we transferred the primary responsibility for marketing the system over to the contracted vendor. The vendor would operate the system at-risk, meaning that they did not

Hire the pros and make the investment you need for the size and quality of the service you plan to launch and operate. Bigger is better in nodal systems.

make money after the initial ramp-up period if the bike-share system didn't generate net profits. This was viewed as a big motivator to get every detail of the marketing mix right and align the city's interests and incentives with that of the private sector. The city was eager to see the system be very popular with the public, but also ideally wanted to have zero operating costs incurred by the taxpayers after the initial capitalization, which had been 80 percent paid for by the federal government and 20 percent by the City of Chicago. The vendor wanted to make a profit and was thus motivated to aggressively market the system, hit local membership and tourist daily-use targets, and meet or surpass their overall revenue goals.

We hired IDEO, an internationally respected and innovative branding firm, to work on the look and feel for what ultimately became Divvy bike share. IDEO challenged us to get really creative in our branding. They realized that "bike share" didn't need to be front and center as part of the name, because it was already a well-known service by 2013. After an extended, collaborative creative process and countless conversations, we chose the striking baby blue from the Chicago flag as the color, Divvy as the name (by definition: to divide and share), and bike sharrow symbols as the accompanying graphic that would accent the fender and the basket on the front. Firebelly Design, a top-flight graphics firm, worked on the logos and accompanying palette of colors, the graphics and picture-heavy website, as well as the design for the redistribution vans, advertisements, uniforms, and merchandise. Pricing was set for members and casual users to maximize uptake and profitability, and we announced the new service opening during Bike to Work Week for maximum impact and to much fanfare. After a cautious and gradual launch, we sold two thousand elite memberships with special black keys.

When launching a service that will become an integral part of a city's transportation network, it is important to let the public play a big role in the planning process. In D.C., we let the public pick the name of the system and also give input on station locations. In Chicago, we took the planning process one step further and hired the top-flight civic data firm Open Plans to design a station crowdsourcing website, as New York had done for their bike-share system. The

Chicago Divvy bikes (Chicago Bicycle Program)

Red Eye Chicago Divvy headline (Gabe Klein)

website gave citizens an opportunity to pinpoint desired station locations on an interactive map, giving them direct input in the planning process, while creating an immense data pool for the system's planners and designers. In addition to this crowdsourcing platform, the city used social media to engage the public. The website is still in use today and was used for the 2015 expansion of Divvy by 175 stations, making it the largest system by stations and land coverage in the United States as of this writing. Through these efforts, we informed potential customers about the features, advantages, and benefits of the system, a critical component of the marketing mix because bike share was new in Chicago and not intuitive for many prospective users who had not used it elsewhere.

We also tried to extend the Divvy brand and make our marketing efforts fun and engaging. Shortly after the system launched, we started a covert campaign featuring a single red bike (in a sea of baby blue). Customers who found, rode, and photographed "Divvy Red" were encouraged to post pictures on social media sites with the hashtag #DivvyRed. Within the first few months of the Divvy launch, we not only were able to get the public heavily involved by gamifying the interactions, but made the brand fun and playful while still communicating the value proposition of bike share as a reliable, inexpensive, super-convenient, and high-quality transportation option for everyone. Our marketing efforts helped us to win over a city that is often, and understandably, skeptical of government and its offerings. From day one, I was happy to see people of all ages and ethnicities using Divvy to get around the city. The marketing team at Divvy and our in-house CDOT bike and public relations team worked seamlessly to engage daily with the press, and to proactively place positive stories about the service, including the first Divvy wedding (which is now a thing) and a story about a group of people who did the Chicago Triathlon on Divvy bikes (now that's crazy!).

Involve the public as much as you can so that they feel ownership and give you valuable input. It is their system.

Customers who found, rode, and photographed "Divvy Red" were encouraged to post pictures on social media sites.

Market just like the best in the private sector. Set a goal to be as good as your hero company, whether Starbucks, Virgin, Tom's Shoes, or—Divvy!

The verdict was in—Chicago loved Divvy. All of our hard work paid off, and there were very few detractors. In Chicago, that's a feat. Before a group of his senior staff, Mayor Emanuel said that Divvy set the standard for a service launch for his administration. I was really proud of our management team, the bike team, and all of our contractors, including the planners who had worked together in public and private partnership to make this happen. I had learned a lot, too. Equally important, there seemed to be less of a "bike stigma" as a result. Outside of some pushback from a thin slice of Chicagoans, and the typical auto-centric folks, the feeling was not that this service was for one group or another. There was a recognition that Divvy was good for everyone.

Get to equity as fast as possible by launching a high-quality, profitable service that everyone wants and is financially sustainable.

Walking for safe streets on new pedestrian crossing in downtown Chicago. (Metropolitan Planning Council)

Most people seemed to understand that like any new transit system, it had to grow, and that we had not reached certain neighborhoods yet. We followed the traditional sharing economy model of launching in the densest areas of the city first to build demand, as we had with Zipcar. The positive here was that people started writing, calling, tweeting, and entering on the website that they wanted Divvy stations in less dense, often less affluent neighborhoods. In 2015, up to 250 more stations are earmarked for installation around Chicagoland, and the system will become regional, like Capital Bikeshare. With this expansion, many traditionally underserved neighborhoods, such as Englewood on the south side of Chicago, will finally get service. The positive side of this strategy? Instead of people feeling that something was being foisted upon them, or that this was part of some scheme to gentrify their neighborhood, we had community members asking us to bring Divvy to them. Using this demand-based strategy helped service to take hold and become a part of the neighborhood fabric and character, not only adding transportation options for people, but also adding a sense of place, and a sense of pride and fairness that every neighborhood is deserving of the most up-to-date services.

What should you do?

- Hire the pros and make the investment you need for the size and quality of the service you plan to launch and operate. Bigger is better in nodal systems.
- Involve the public as much as you can so that they feel ownership and give you valuable input. It is their system.
- Market just like the best in the private sector. Set a goal to be as good as your hero company, whether Starbucks, Virgin, Tom's Shoes, or—Divvy!
- Get to equity as fast as possible by launching a high-quality, profitable service that everyone wants and is financially sustainable.

Envisioning Zero

In the United States, we lose more than 32,000 people each year to traffic crashes, including 4,500–5,000 pedestrians. We chalk these deaths up to the cost of having automobiles. In a conversation with world-renowned urban designer Jan Gehl, he explained to me the outrage of the Danes in the late 1960s, when the auto-centric movement in Europe started to claim the lives of children, some of the most vulnerable citizens of our cities. Gehl was right there in the middle of it and played a key role in leveraging that anger to transform the culture back toward one that prioritized walking, cycling, transit, and experiencing cities at human scale. At the heart of this philosophy was valuing of life, health, and happiness over efficiency of travel or mode, specifically the automobile. The Danes made a concerted effort to change, to fix the damage, to remove excess car lanes and parking, and to replace them with spaces for people.

Applying a continuous process improvement philosophy to traffic crashes of all types, we are an abysmal failure. Worldwide, 1.24 million people die on the roads each year. More than 70 percent of the fatalities are in developing countries, and 50 percent of that total involve our most vulnerable citizens—our young, our old, our disabled. This is absolutely inexcusable. Like alcoholism, the first step is a recognition that there is a problem. But in America, we are still not there.

The Vision Zero movement in Sweden, which set an aggressive goal of zero fatalities on their roads by 2020, was passed by parliament in 1997. That mission arose out of the same Northern European culture that Jan Gehl comes from, as well as a recognition that there are no "accidents," only institutional failures resulting in "crashes" that take people's lives and make city streets feel like a game of Frogger instead of the safe and connected places that they should be.

Sweden has a wide-ranging plan to reach this goal, from safety improvements and better technology in automobiles, to redesigning streets for slower speeds and active transportation, to automated enforcement campaigns that not only ticket speeders, but register law-abiding citizens automatically to win a percentage of the speeding ticket revenues, every week! The Swedes are experimenting with employing behavioral economics to gamify a problem and make it fun to be safer. I was determined, along with my team,[1] to take aspects of

Vision Zero and apply them to Chicago's mean streets in a way that would make a difference. Chicago adopted the Vision Zero approach in 2012 and has been followed by many other major cities, including New York, San Francisco, and Los Angeles.

Before we went public with our Complete Streets plan for Chicago, our policy and planning unit decided to adopt a Vision Zero policy for the city, stating that we wanted to get to zero traffic deaths in our city by 2022. Some of you may wonder why or how we thought we could get from 125 deaths a year, with more than a quarter of that from pedestrians, to zero without some monumental changes. On top of re-engineering of city streets and comprehensive education of the public, we ramped up our red-light camera program and passed legislation for a full-fledged automated enforcement program, with speed cameras, to make big changes over the ten-year period. Our Vision Zero goal hit the ground just as Chicago's "Be Safe, Be Alert" education campaign launched, which we worked to brand as a powerful and emotionally salient marketing tool.

The campaign went through several iterations. The first draft that the team and our consultants brought forward smacked of a promotion for an outdated government program. The materials were far more focused on distracted walking and paying attention to cars rather than communicating a message that could grab the attention of both drivers and pedestrians and shake them to their core. Something often overlooked by city agencies or their private-sector partners is the huge amount of advertising assets available to them. From city-owned billboards, subway stations, the interior and exterior of buses and subway cars, to the public space itself and even our trash cans, we aimed to use all of these untapped assets to stem the tide of injuries and fatalities on our streets. To do that, we needed a campaign worthy of the assets we were going to use, and it needed to be powerful in imagery.

One morning, while we were working on this project, I was told that a speeding car had hit an eight-year-old boy as he stepped off of the sidewalk on his way to school. He survived, but his foot had been run over and would likely be amputated. The driver fled, as they often do in Chicago. This terrible incident, and the fact that it was barely newsworthy, reinforced my resolve. I told my team that I wanted graphic imagery of the reality of the carnage and damage created by this kind of behavior front and center in the campaign. The pedestrian team pushed back initially and felt that it was too controversial and too negative, potentially turning people off. But we weren't marketing bike-share memberships; we were changing bad behavior that permanently altered the course of people's lives. We aimed to take a culture of acceptance of these preventable crashes as "accidents" and forge a culture of intolerance and activism.

We called our new campaign "It's Up To You." It featured a mother, son, daughter, and other people important in everyone's lives. We used intense imagery of the aftermath of crashes—these failures of our system and fallible people—combined with messages highlighting that this could be your loved one, in order to make it personal. Our goal was to create a culture of personal responsibility in the city of Chicago and increase awareness of traffic deaths as a preventable problem with tangible solutions.

To reinforce the focus that these were real lives, and not just statistics, we came up with the idea of using public space to bring the thirty-two pedestrians killed in the previous year back to our streets to remind others of the sacrifice they were forced to make due to these accepted "accidents." I initially wanted to recruit my friend Marc Jenkins, a well-known artist who creates installations featuring imaginary "tape people" in public space. Marc was not available, but we used his ideas and dressed thirty-two mannequins in Vision Zero shirts that let the public know they represented Chicagoans who had been victims of traffic crashes. We launched the campaign on the busiest thoroughfare in the city, Wacker Drive, just as the weather was warming.

There were, of course, a few hiccups. The first morning of the campaign, I received a call that one of the mannequins on State Street, a busy shopping and commuter thoroughfare, had had his pants pulled down and was mooning the passersby at rush hour. To prevent this from happening again, we permanently glued on each mannequin's pants. Despite a few small, sometimes funny setbacks, the project was a major success and got a tremendous amount of press.

We launched Vision Zero in 2012 and saw a 7.5-percent decrease in fatalities in 2013, while the state, which had been fighting us on many of our progressive safety initiatives, saw an increase in road deaths.

For all of our projects and initiatives, whether on our websites, on social media, or in interviews, we proactively sold the public on a cohesive vision for the future. Then we delivered on time and on budget. We also worked to get the best return on investment that we could for the taxpayers while straining the

Components of the Vision Zero safety initiative in Chicago, including (a) mannequins, (b) stickers, and (c) ads
(a, c: Michelle Stenzel, Bike Walk Lincoln Park; b: Metropolitan Planning Council)

public finance system as little as possible. There are always going to be detractors and naysayers no matter what you do, but if you make sure that you are proactively putting as much information in front of people as possible, reaching out to involve them, and educating them on the benefits of your initiative, you multiply your chances of success exponentially.

What should you do?

- Admit that you have a problem. Find positive, realistic ways to solve it.
- Don't be afraid to set an audacious goal that seems too difficult to achieve. Nothing great is ever easy to do.
- Take your audacious goal and break it down into manageable milestones in a reasonable time frame.
- Make the public a partner in your mission by showing them the personal and practical impacts on people's lives of the problem at hand.
- Lead: make the difficult choices to address the problem, whether speed cameras, speed limit reductions, or serious penalties if injuries or death result from negligence.
- Measure your performance and always reevaluate the levers that are most effective to achieve your goals.

Notes

1   Luann Hamilton, who headed up planning and project development; Janet Attarian, who ran Complete Streets; Kiersten Grove, our pedestrian coordinator; and many others got aggressive with our plans.

Press conference to launch the new Chicago street safety initiative in 2013 (Metropolitan Planning Council)

Lesson #5

Ross Barney Architects (Architect), Sasaki Associates (Landscape Architect), Alfred Benesch & Co. (Engineering), Jacobs Ryan Associates (Landscape Architect), Schuler & Shook (Lighting Design)

Fund Creatively

On how to find funding where none seemingly exists, make the most of a slim budget, and get creative with the basics

Y ou can have the best ideas, the most beautiful plans, and your stakeholder buy-in all lined up, but if you can't figure out a way ultimately to fund your ambitious projects, then it's all for naught in my book. Now don't get me wrong, I am not saying that you have to know your funding source for every project when you start out—quite the opposite. Almost no businesses would get off the ground if this were the case. The Chicago Riverwalk project is a great example of this. We had a vision, and we knew that we could find the money if the conceptual design grabbed and excited our stakeholders, but we didn't have our funding figured out at the start. To be honest, we really didn't have a funding plan at all. But our team within CDOT, our CFO's office, and our federal government relations team in D.C. worked together and figured out an innovative public-private financing scheme to make the project happen. I have never had to stop an initiative (that I can remember) because of a dead end on funding—from my food truck company, to car leases at Zipcar, to Chicago's $365-million 11th Street bridges, two bike-share programs, the Bloomingdale Trail, one hundred miles

Bloomingdale Trail proposed ramp (Framework design team: Arup, Ross Barney Architects, Michael Van Valkenburgh Associates, Chicago Public Art Group)

of bike lanes, and on and on. There is a way to go about assessing your financial levers once you enter an organization, then creatively figuring out how to fund your initiatives.

Here are a few basic steps for how to assess your finances when walking into a new organization:

1. *Determine your sources and uses of cash now*

What is your cash on hand? How much of it has already been allocated to nonnegotiable projects? Getting to know your budget, no matter if you are in the public or private sector, is absolutely critical. Knowledge is power, and it's not just about knowing the numbers, but what is behind them. How does the bulk of your revenue come in? For what is it typically designated? Do you run a deficit, or have a profit? Is your cash flow seasonal?

In Washington, D.C., DDOT had a great funding mechanism called the "unified fund" put in place by Dan Tangherlini in the mid-2000s. Our budget directors, Matt Brown, and later Leah Treat, who now runs Portland's Bureau of Transportation, taught me how it worked and how to work it. Like any DOT, we had a large capital budget for building projects, and an operating budget for everything from filling potholes and paying salaries to running services like Capital Bikeshare. The unified fund was what's known as an "enterprise fund." In essence, its brilliance is in its private-sector roots because the fund allowed us to "eat what we killed." If we implemented a more-efficient parking program that generated significantly more revenue and saved on operating costs because of the efficiency of new technologies like pay-by-phone (which we did), DDOT kept that money and we could reinvest it into our own programs. Now this may seem normal to many of you reading this, but it is actually unusual for cities to have a dedicated reinvestment stream for an agency or for infrastructure, beyond a local gas tax. In most cases, all new revenues generated go into a general fund and are reallocated by the executive through the main budget office with legislative approval.

When the unified fund was created in the early 2000s, the city had the foresight to recognize that transportation was similar to a utility and required a permanent, consistent, and predictable funding source over time. Cities already suffer from excessive turnover in the executive ranks due to the nature of political cycles and because leadership often comes and goes with the mayor. This frustrates consistent planning and execution. The unified fund helped to maintain consistency for long-range planning and execution across administrations. Similar to the highway trust fund at the federal level, Dan and Mayor Anthony Williams recognized that without sustainable resources over the long term, day-to-day funding would depend on the whims of political cycles and one-time infusions through appropriations. For those of us working in the agency, the basic premise stood that any entity that derived a measurable benefit from its use of the public right-of-way could and should be charged a fee for its usage. Those fees went back into the enterprise fund, thereby creating a self-financing mechanism for the agency, which we used for local initiatives and as a match for federal formula funds. As a result, we were able to create entrepreneurs within DDOT who stood to reap the benefits of their own work internally to fund future projects. We had tremendous assets that could be leveraged to bring in revenues, from parking meters and cafe sidewalk space to service sponsorships and street furniture contracts. Taking stock of these assets becomes very important if they are *the* key financing mechanism to fulfill your team's goals. If you can work with your stakeholders to enable a mechanism to capture the value of improvements made to the system, getting things done and motivating your team becomes easier.

2.   *Lay out your vision and dedicate budget to it*

Whether coming into a new business unit or a government agency, it's crucial to quickly learn the current state of affairs, then set priorities clearly and make sure that they represent what your leader (mayor/CEO/director) values. Once you assess your leader's needs, and account for the projects or initiatives that have been programmed prior to your arrival and need to come to fruition, allocate budget for those priorities first. Cash flow is important here. Let's say that you have a $50-million bridge project, but you are one year behind in the planning or design, and once you undertake the project it will take twenty-four months to complete. This may have looked like a $50-million need in 2016, but when you dig into it, it's more like $25 million needed in 2017 and $25 million in 2018. For a federally funded project, you need to show that all of the budget is in place prior to obligating it in a fiscally restrained plan. As a result, you may have just found $25 million each in 2016 and 2017 that you can use now for a newer initiative. Once you've completed this cash flow analysis, you can identify uncommitted funds that might be used for your key initiatives and discretionary pilot projects.

The next step is to do the math and figure out the shortfalls for your initiatives, after which you can figure out new sources of revenue or how funding can be flexed from a lower priority toward a new initiative. This is how the Chicago Riverwalk project happened. Some of the early money for soft costs such as design and engineering came from other projects that were behind their original timeline, or projects that came in under budget, freeing up dollars that when pieced together became quite significant. Then we brainstormed ways to figure out the larger capital plan, which included innovative finance options and incentives aligned with private stakeholders.

Ideally, your vision and goals should be clearly spelled out and broken down into manageable qualitative milestones in a published action agenda or yearly plan. This should be associated with your quantitative goals and fiscal year budget, including revenue and expenditure targets. Once completed, your qualitative plan, linked internally to the finance plan, can be circulated to all management and staff, ideally becoming a formal document signed by the mayor or CEO and made required reading for personnel. Following up with in-person meetings to answer questions about the goals and the agreed-upon milestones is a good idea for leadership in the responsible agency or division. This ensures that team members are brought back into the tent again following action agenda planning, and that strategizing on funding gaps and the ways to overcome them and execute the projects becomes a team effort.

3. *Spread profit and loss (P&L) responsibility as widely as possible*

I have learned that if managers are not accountable for profits or losses within their area of responsibility, then they can lose their sense of ownership, and in turn, their awareness of the importance of fiscal responsibility and return on investment (ROI). Staff will then certainly lose a sense of connection between driving top-line revenues, bottom-line responsibility, and ultimately, the relationship to the quality of service provided to the customer. Instilling a consciousness of financial metrics and levers helps to set realistic goals and almost always drives a better-quality product or service for the end customer, public or private. Why? Because to meet your financial objectives, you may need to have a higher-quality service and a better marketing mousetrap to get across your value proposition and ensure usage. In a city transportation agency, that means higher-quality parking meters connected to pay-by-phone, better-operated and balanced bike share, the right prices, the right website, smartphone applications, and more. P&L understanding and accountability combined with strong performance management based on quantitative metrics is key. If your team is not bringing in enough revenue or is spending too much, a problem of balance needs to be addressed in a collaborative, continuous process improvement–oriented environment.

4.   *Establish a formal budgeting process*

For your team to feel that they have "agreed upon" S.M.A.R.T. goals, budgeting must be an integral and collaborative effort. In a perfect world, individual teams are responsible for setting their own goals, and these goals fit into the larger construct within the agency or company. No matter how small or large an organization, this is a critical tenet of effective budgeting. If you are the director of CDOT, you need to set goals for how much asphalt you will need to fill the estimated number of potholes based on historical trends, just as if you are the owner of the asphalt plant, you would need to gauge how much asphalt you are going to sell. Both sides need to establish budgets and goals associated with them, understanding, of course, that contingency plans should be developed for aberrations (as in D.C.'s Snowmageddon in 2010, in which our agency spent more than $40 million!). Once the high-level goal has been approximated, the assumptions need to be tested by managers in the trenches to ensure that they are realistic. Ideally, those team members on the front line set the ultimate metrics and they filter up to management for agreement, rather than management imposing them in a top-down fashion. Regardless, you want the entire organization paddling in the same direction, and this takes both qualitative *and* quantitative goal setting and leadership, along with organizational consensus building and agreed-upon metrics and goals.

5. *Recognize the importance of return on investment (ROI)*

I often hear people say "that's too expensive" when they disagree with an idea, either philosophically or because it's in their backyard. At the federal level, we regularly hear political representatives say that we can't afford to pay for workers' healthcare, raise the minimum wage, or fund social programs. The same people think spending hundreds of billions of dollars on defense in foreign lands is just fine. So let's face it, these sentiments aren't about fiscal responsibility as much they are about fiscal preferences and programmatic priorities. So when people told me, "the streetcar costs too much," "the bus rapid transit system costs too much," or "how can we afford the new riverwalk?," I always had the same response: What's the return on investment? Cities need to be good stewards of public money, but they also need to work to get the best value on the dollar. For instance, if we spend $1.6 billion on a streetcar network in Washington, D.C., but the estimates are that the city will see more than $8 billion dollars of return from that project, based on an intensive land use study—a fivefold ROI by one measure alone—then I feel that there is a pretty strong case to justify that project cost. In this case, it is also helpful to look at the estimated tax dollars generated for the municipal coffers from new real estate, new residents, and new jobs. These resources can collectively be enough to pay off the bond issuance that funds the project. In another example, if I am going to spend 50 percent more on each pothole filled in D.C. using a more expensive material, with no additional efficiencies (such as more potholes filled per hour), and the mitigation lasts only 20 percent longer than the current material, then I am looking at a negative return on my investment, so no go. That said, if a new technology or service costing 20 percent more enables me to get five times as many potholes filled in the same amount of time and cuts my labor overhead by more than 50 percent, then we might have a real winner.

You need to have a strong filter for screening what's worth investing in. No project should move forward without being examined for its ROI. Now for the reality: ROI can be very complicated to calculate in the public sector, because there may be intangible benefits that have real upside to government, such as equity considerations, for instance, or moving people from a transportation mode with more greenhouse gas emissions to zero-emission bicycles. I would argue that you can actually quantify these benefits to society, and that you need to do so if you are going to break even from revenues tied to operations alone. Studies actually show that for every dollar spent on a bike lane, cities receive $6–$24 in future benefit in terms of reduced pollution, lower vehicle congestion, increased health, and fewer deaths. Find a way to standardize your approach to ROI and quantify what many today see as intangible benefits, and you'll find that the return for a lot of your projects can reinforce your future investments and guide smart decision-making.[1]

Now for a slight contradiction. You have to diversify your portfolio. You would never put your entire personal investment portfolio in bonds with a 4-percent safe return when the S&P 500 is returning 13 percent annually and technology funds are returning close to 20 percent.[2] Well, it's the same thing from an infrastructure finance perspective. Paving roads is equivalent to putting your money in bonds. These are hefty capital expenditures with lower returns over a long period than a bike lane, a parklet, or new parking meters, which can produce considerably higher ROI and immediate returns. When mapping out your returns on investment, make sure to weigh them based on the amount of cash you are putting in relative to the return. Of course, I am not saying that you shouldn't pave roads—quite the contrary. But I am arguing that you should not be putting your budget only into expensive, heavy infrastructure. Diversifying my portfolio and generating revenues from public space to reinvest in softer infrastructure and services has been key to my success.

The example of bike lanes in Chicago

In 2011, we set an ambitious goal to install one hundred miles of protected bike lanes in Chicago. This level of commitment was unheard of at the time, and it had the potential to establish a new precedent for cities around the country because we were committing to miles of *protected* bike lanes, rather than conventional on-street bike lanes, which rarely require removing lanes and shifting parking spaces.

Before the mayor announced that I was assuming leadership of the CDOT in his new administration and we were fine-tuning the mayor's verbal commitments, I actually got cold feet and scratched out the term "protected" and left "bike lanes," because I and others knew that it would, practically speaking, be

Chicago protected bike lane

almost impossible to finance, plan, and install one hundred miles of protected bike lanes in the proposed time frame (this is two hundred "lane miles," actually, which is how many cities count their installations). Plus, differing road widths would dictate different configurations block by block, eliminating separation at various points. We would be subject to the state's strict roadway design guidelines within their jurisdiction and where we were using federal funds. At the press conference, Mayor Emanuel paused when he saw what I had scratched out. He then decided to overrule me and stated our goal as "one hundred miles of protected bike lanes." Internally, I felt a mixture of anguish and excitement. There was no funding committed to this goal and, on top of that, I would soon learn that those who controlled the purse strings ultimately were not committed to the plan. This put me in an awkward position: I had to clash with people in control of the city budget to let me build the bike lanes that the mayor had mandated. The odds were not in our favor.

When you work in a political environment, and things can be just as political in the private as the public sector, you have to learn to straddle fences. In this instance, it was my incredibly creative and bright staff, led by Luann Hamilton and Scott Kubly in our project development group, our traffic engineering team, and my managing deputy and money wiz, Leah Treat in finance, who played the foil with the purse strings and figured out how to fund the mayor's mandate.

With our aggressive goal out in the open, we installed our first protected bike lane within thirty days of Mayor Emanuel taking office. To do it, we begged, we borrowed, and we stole from other line items. We scraped together a few thousand dollars from paving and striping, used in-house forces wherever possible, and due to the tight time frame, our internal CDOT bike team, along with the Active Transportation Alliance, went door to door educating people about the project. The local alderman jumped in as a result and helped us convince his constituents of the project's worth. The SRAM Fund, an arm of the SRAM bicycle corporation based in Chicago and led by longtime cycling activist Randy Neufeld, donated $15,000 worth of thermoplastic marking material to the project so we could finish it. The CDOT bike team, led by longtime bike coordinator Ben Gomberg, came together and banged out the details every day to meet the thirty-day goal. We wanted everyone in the city to see how fast one lane could go in, and to glean the immediate positive effects before the season went away. The next year, we had to install twenty-five miles to stay on track for our goal.

Over the course of 2011 and into 2012, we spent eight months doing outreach to every corner of the city. Through this outreach, our planning and bike teams, along with Sam Schwartz Engineering, put together the Chicago Streets for Cycling Plan 2020.[3] The plan called for 645 miles of bike facilities in Chicago, or a high-quality facility within a half mile of every Chicagoan. Nonetheless, we still had no dedicated budget to actually implement the plan, and I didn't want to let the mayor know how much internal strife we were facing from the budget office, so we had to go it alone. For 2014 and 2015, we planned to use federal Congestion Mitigation Air Quality funds, the same federal funding that we planned to use for bike share. How? We realized there were lower priority projects that we could push out, fund differently, or bring in under budget in the future. But

A young Chicagoan helps with bike lane construction (Chicago Bicycle Program)

for 2012 and 2013, we had nothing. Federal grants require extensive paperwork and processing, so it's hard to get the money right away, even if you are assured the funds by your regional metropolitan planning organization. At the same time, we received hardly any local money from the budget office. So we opted to do a few strategic things to make the mayor's bike program start to come to fruition immediately:

- Now that we had a citywide plan, we overlaid the bike plan on streets already in the paving schedule to "piggyback" and roll the costs of paving and striping together.
- We were paving more arterial streets now than we had in a decade by changing the surface depth of our contract paving to stretch our funds significantly, almost double, to get to more roads. This translated to more bike lane opportunities.
- We appealed to aldermen who supported bike infrastructure to use some of their discretionary funds to help fill gaps in the funding for smaller items like bollards for separating bikes from cars. As we spread to more neighborhoods, more aldermen started calling us to ask how they could get more bike lanes. In this way, we gradually built up support through the visible advertising of the expanding network, as well as the political consciousness of local politicians eager to keep pace with neighboring wards.

- We pushed hard on the budget office and were able to get budget for basic lane striping, which was absolutely necessary and a safety concern when we took office. This budget, which was still insufficient to do all of the striping we needed to do, was helpful in getting bike facilities in as we restriped streets.
- We started to hold utilities, and to a lesser extent, developers, to a much higher standard for full-width restorations of streets where they did work. This coordination developed into a ledger system that allowed the city and the private sector to benefit by sharing costs, or trading project restorations. This kept mobilization costs down and tax dollars spent to a minimum. This also translated to more bike lane miles being installed.

And it worked! Some people wondered about the order of the projects we were choosing and the overall connectivity in the short term, but we ultimately wanted and needed to have enough geographic reach to engage diverse parts of the city, and our strategy accomplished that. In our first two years, with essentially zero dedicated budget, we hit all of our milestones and built half of the network until the federal money finally came in.

Miracle? It felt like it, but no. It was the smarts and dedication of a team that would not take "no" for an answer. At any time, it would have been easy to give up in the face of seemingly insurmountable odds, but this is not what social en-

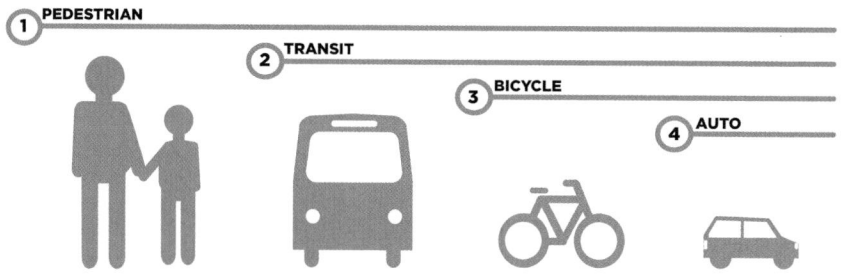

Pedestrian-first modal hierarchy from the 2013 Complete Streets plan for Chicago by the Chicago Department of Transportation (Farr Associates & Nelson Nygaard)

trepreneurs do. We persevered on behalf of the people. Although funding availability alone should not dictate whether you pursue a project, it does ultimately determine whether or not it gets built. In many ways, our approach to the bike program in Chicago reflects the typical approach used by private-sector startups. We bootstrapped the program until the larger grant dollars came in for later years. In so doing, we kept our costs to a minimum, forgoing additional contracts and salaries and using revenues to incrementally grow the program, just as an entrepreneur would until they could line up debt or equity financing in the private sector. This approach to public financing allowed greater flexibility in the short term, enabling us to undertake more innovative projects from the project development process all the way to the implementation phase.

What should you do?

- You must sell your vision, internally and externally, up and down, to get buy-in and the associated budget. It's best to put your vision on paper and make it as public as possible once your boss signs off.
- Have a formal budgeting process and push it as far down in the organization as possible. Everyone should be aware of what's at stake, and how every dollar spent affects the ultimate product or service for the consumer.
- Ideally, you want to be able to generate revenues to incentivize entrepreneurial spirit and to add understanding of the value of your assets and services. Work with your bosses to create the ability to self-fund your programs as much as possible. More control means more empowered people and faster, more flexible action.
- Don't worry about how much an initiative "costs" in the abstract. Focus on whether there is an adequate return on that investment, whether a 1-mile bike lane or a 50-mile streetcar system.
- Where there is a will, there is a way to fund it. If you have that attitude, the people who work for you and with you will, too. Never give up.

Notes

1   For example, http://journalistsresource.org/studies/environment/transportation/societal-costs-benefits-commuter-bicycling

2   NASDAQ QQQ exchange-traded funds in 2014.

3   http://chicagobikes.org/pdf/2012 Projects/ChicagoStreetsforCycling2020.pdf

Lesson #6

(Kevin Kovaleski)

Bridge the Public-Private Divide

On forging a proactive bureaucracy and making life better for everyone in the process

On August 13, 2014, the City of Boston held a public hearing on a controversial new mobile application called Haystack. Haystack, an on-demand parking application modeled on Uber, had launched in Boston only twelve days before at a lavish party described by one journalist as something out of the HBO sitcom *Silicon Valley*. The twenty-four-year-old CEO Eric Meyer found himself at odds over the app with City of Boston legislators within a matter of days. He struggled to refute accusations that the app was profiting off public space, as opposed to selling "information" about parking space availability. At the hearing for legislation banning the app, Meyer warned the city that "to prohibit the app would be a signal from the city against innovation," calling the decision "ominous" for young entrepreneurs such as himself involved in the city's nascent tech scene.

Haystack's demise, although a caricatured portrait of private- and public-sector dynamics, provides a window into how their interests can stand at odds, and why the two sides now need to understand one another's perspective more

By understanding the incentives and the cultures that drive each side, the public and private sectors can partner more constructively, and ultimately, work together to create better cities.

than ever, rather than work against one another. By monetizing government property, in the eyes of the city, Haystack failed to see the city's basic obligation to ensure fair and equal access to public space. The city, meanwhile, was not prepared with a comprehensive vision for how to collaborate and leverage private-sector mobile technologies to increase parking turnover and revenue and make life better for citizens.

So far in the book, I have devoted a lot of room to discussing how to infuse the public sector with the urgency and energy of a startup. Now, I want to shift my focus toward how to bridge the divide between the private and the public sectors. My goal here is to demonstrate that by understanding the incentives and the cultures that drive each side, the public and private sectors can partner more constructively, and ultimately, work together to create better cities. This chapter begins with a discussion of Zipcar as an example of a successful partnership with government and ends with a discussion of D.C.'s Capital Bikeshare system as a successful partnership, led by the government, with the private sector.

Zipcar: Private-public collaboration

When I joined Robin Chase at Zipcar at the end of 2002 as regional vice president in the Washington, D.C. region, the company was still tiny. We had twenty-eight vehicles in D.C. three employees, and I would estimate, a few thousand customers total across the three cities in which we operated at the time (Cambridge/Boston, New York, and D.C.). Our main competitor, Flexcar, was a West Coast company that had launched in D.C. in partnership with the Washington Metropolitan Area Transit Authority, a.k.a. Metro, the local transit system. Metro had a formal partnership with Flexcar and would not give Zipcar the time of day. Our Seattle-based competitors seemed to have car sharing vehicles at every Metro station with an available parking lot, but were lacking density of vehicles in the city, as was Zipcar in its earliest incarnation.

At the time, most of the stations with Flexcars were suburban, because those were the Metro locations with spacious park-and-ride lots, even though, based on our research, the biggest demand for car sharing was in the densest areas of the urban core, where parking was most difficult. City dwellers, especially those

Although we take car sharing for granted today, at that time, it was a new idea—not a slam-dunk value proposition by any means.

without cars or with only one car to a household, were most willing to try this new type of service. Keep in mind that in the early days of car sharing, gas was hovering around $1.25 per gallon and people had only recently started streaming back into the city centers and their surrounding, older neighborhoods.

Although we take car sharing for granted today, at that time, it was a new idea—not a slam-dunk value proposition by any means. Zipcar prided itself on its entrepreneurship and was proud to operate without government sponsorship like Flexcar had. Because of that, we had to work harder, market ourselves more aggressively, and fight for the most desirable parking lots and individual spaces for our vehicles. Like Uber and Lyft today, supply and demand were the name of the game, and matching the two represented the holy grail.

Over a number of years, we fine-tuned an internal planning system that broke every city down by neighborhood and then census tract, then drilled into the density data by block, car ownership, transit ridership, parking availability, median price, and other factors. Once we decided to enter or grow a geography, we applied an extremely rigorous and well-timed marketing plan, over which we laid out our vehicle plan. Our strategy was to create the demand and then increase the supply very carefully to maximize profits and minimize customer frustration. At the time, Flexcar, in my opinion, was far too reliant on its government partnership, and was not terribly responsive to customer needs. As we started ramping up our vehicle fleet with new vehicle types, including pickup trucks for hauling and convertibles for fun, Flexcar remained relatively stagnant and committed to hybrid Honda Civics in less

Flexcar in dedicated spot (Disavian on Wikimedia Commons)

Zipcar in dedicated spot (Deanlaw on Wikimedia Commons)

dense areas, addressing the "last mile" solution rather than catering to multi-modal users in the urban core.

While they were busy fulfilling their contract with Metro, we locked up all five universities in Washington, D.C., under a contract for parking on campus, marketing to students and securing corporate accounts. Meanwhile, I partnered with Flexcar to work on an on-street parking program with Arlington County that we later expanded to Washington, D.C.'s city streets. Some senior management at Zipcar was opposed to this, and Flexcar was surprised that we would initiate such a partnership. By that time, though, we already had the upper hand, so I saw no reason not to work together to make car sharing an extension of the public transportation system. The key to beating Flexcar was to be better in every way we could, but most importantly, to attack on every front versus just falling back on the prospect of public-sector support. In a nutshell, we needed to be able to operate profitably with no government support.

Arlington, Virginia, an extremely progressive "urban village" adjacent to Washington, D.C., had an innovative, risk-taking transportation culture and little patience for bureaucracy. Chris Hamilton led (and continues to lead, as of this writing) the city's transportation demand management efforts as Arlington County commuter services chief. Chris not only wanted to place car sharing on the streets in dedicated spaces around the city, but he wanted to make it happen with both companies in less than ninety days! A month or so after the Arlington launch, I met with Dan Tangherlini, who ran the D.C. Department of Transportation (DDOT) at that time. Dan asked

The city's equity requirement ended up teaching us an important lesson—that your perceived market is not always your actual market, and that there is a lot to be gained by both the city and private companies in diversifying your geographic reach and taking an unconventional approach. By engaging with the private sector, the government shaped the rollout of the service, ensuring equity and data sharing, and that we worked for the greater good.

me why Zipcar had done its original pilot with Arlington County rather than D.C. The reality was that Arlington was open to doing the pilot, and doing it quickly. Dan replied, "I like Arlington looking at my back, not looking at theirs, so let's make this happen."

Launching Zipcar in D.C. took more than a year, but when we finally did, there were eighty-three dedicated spaces for car sharing on D.C. city streets to be split between Zipcar and Flexcar. This was a game changer for Zipcar, and for Washington, D.C., as a progressive city. We were now a high profile, government-sanctioned extension of the public transportation system catering to an increasingly multimodal population in the D.C. region's densest neighborhoods rather than to suburban commuters at the Metro's fringe.

At this point, Flexcar, which had failed to reinvent its business model or grasp the coming demographic and cultural shift, was looking at our backs. We owned the urban market. We owned the university market and, on the backs of a recent contract with Metro alongside Flexcar, we had balanced the playing field on the government side. We had also built a fleet of pickup trucks, MINI Coopers, Mazda minivans, and BMWs that were sitting next to their aging Honda Civics. On top of all this, we now had access to free advertising on the subways and buses and in the transit stations as part of the

Zipcar-dedicated space in Washington, D.C.

Metro contract. Our branded vehicles were sitting in public parking spaces all around the city.

As part of the agreement with Metro, we were required to place Zipcars in low-income, less-dense neighborhoods. Although the vehicle use in these areas started out slow, after a short period, our vehicles east of the Anacostia River often produced the highest revenue in the fleet. The city's equity requirement ended up teaching us an important lesson—that your perceived market is not always your actual market, and that there is a lot to be gained by both the city and private companies in diversifying your geographic reach and taking an unconventional approach. By engaging with the private sector, the government shaped the rollout of the service, ensuring equity and data sharing, and that we worked for the greater good.

As Zipcar grew as a whole, we worked to master the operations side of the business. This is where I learned about and used Lean Six Sigma and continuous process improvement techniques to fine-tune the efficiency of an operations-intensive business. In D.C., we even worked with an outside vendor called Kangaroo Car Care to customize their offerings to externally service Zipcar's very specific needs around cleaning, bodywork, and other maintenance. This resulted in the highest customer service scores in the company.

We had two primary issues with government in D.C. proper. The first was that they had no business license for "car sharing," so we were technically operating as a rental-car company. This had to be resolved for our business proposition to work for customers. Otherwise, a one-hour, $8 rental would have had a $9 convention center surcharge, negating the value of the service and the simplicity of the concept. A second obstacle we encountered while working with the government was the registration and taxation of our vehicle fleet. Zipcar was being charged a considerable fee for sales/excise taxes even though our vehicles gave all of the benefits of a hybrid vehicle owned by one person, who would be exempt from taxation for fuel efficiency standards. Our vehicles were shared by hundreds of people, saving much more on fuel and emissions than a typical car or hybrid. After a few conversations with the mayor's office, DDOT, and D.C. Department of Motor Vehicles, we were able to get this tax, which was 6–8 percent per vehicle, waived. The average price of a vehicle is $25,000, and we were in-fleeting one hundred vehicles per year at 7 percent, which translated to $175,000 per year. These cost savings went straight to the bottom line, which in turn allowed us to keep our prices lower for consumers, thereby getting more people to give up their cars and use car sharing. We also were able to get the Department of Consumer and Regulatory Affairs to adopt a new car-sharing business license under which we could operate with standard sales taxation. These two resolutions are examples of win-win-wins for government, the private sector, and the consumer.

The D.C. Zipcar model combined aggressive business development efforts with partners ranging from governments to universities, developers, and even the Washington Nationals baseball team to expand our physical footprint, our marketing reach, and our membership. We also employed aggressive guerrilla marketing to directly reach consumers on the streets, and on a budget. Finally,

. . . competition only makes you better in the long run

we finely tuned and maintained highly efficient operations to stay as competitive as possible, and the D.C. model ultimately became the preferred model for expansion nationally and globally. Zipcar soon purchased Flexcar and became the largest car-sharing company in the world.

There are four takeaways here, but perhaps the most important one is that competition only makes you better in the long run. D.C. was the only market with a car-sharing competitor in the early days, and by most metrics, it was also the most successful city experimenting with car sharing at the time.

Another takeaway is that although government partnership was ultimately very important to Zipcar, we consistently maintained a focus on the customer and responded primarily to those needs. A strong, amicable partnership with government pushed us over the top, helped us scale while keeping marketing costs low, and ultimately made us profitable. Fundamentally, a company needs to have the best quality product or service to win the customer, and to win period. I know what you might be thinking—that it's not government's role to ensure that a private company stays afloat, right? Well, maybe. The alternative would have been for the government to start its own car-sharing program and run this very complex business themselves to get the public benefit. By empowering private companies to make the business work in partnership with the government, the public sector effectively eliminated any financial risk to the taxpayer, fostered a new industry that created jobs, and saw the shedding of so many cars that vehicle registrations dropped by 6 percent in D.C. while the population grew by 3 percent. Why should the government take on something the private sector is willing to do on their own? There are now no less than five car-sharing companies in Washington, D.C., with new peer-to-peer entrants such as Getaround hitting the market this year. This is a direct result of an entrepreneurial government fostering a smart public-private partnership in the interest of their mutual consumers. Moreover, following this success, D.C. now charges market rates to the car-sharing companies for parking.

Takeaway three is that the urban core is the most viral place to grow a business because of its density and energy. By sticking to last-mile suburban commuter stops, Flexcar missed the big opportunity standing right in front of them.

And the final takeaway: even though we don't typically think this way, governments are also in competition. As a private-sector manager, I tended to think of government as slow, bureaucratic, and monopolistic. Although I learned that this remains the case in many places, there are people such as Chris Hamilton and his team in Arlington County, Virginia, who have the ambition and the ability to make change happen quickly. Finding those people helped to create demand for more change elsewhere in the region, and ultimately nationally.

The Capital Bikeshare story:
Public-private collaboration

When I took over at DDOT, I was intrigued with the new SmartBike program that had launched in D.C. just prior to my arrival. SmartBike was the first bike share program in North America. Although only a small fraction of the size of the successful European bike-sharing systems at the time (one hundred as opposed to a few thousand bikes), and perhaps even dinkier in terms of the bikes themselves, the concept was right up my alley.

Some people say that the SmartBike program was a failure, but I beg to differ. The system was a pilot with an uninterested vendor, and unfortunately or fortunately, depending on how you choose to look at it, it was too small at ten stations and one hundred bikes to work well as a transit system. The public got a taste of what a system like this could be, although neither the city nor its private partner, the mass media company Clear Channel, invested heavily enough in what quickly became antiquated technology and required capital construction to implement at scale.

Having said that, from the moment I set foot in my new job, I was excited to grow the program. When I was finally able to come up for air after my first few weeks at DDOT, I started to talk to the bike division about the public-private partnership that had resulted in SmartBike. As it turns out, like the much larger Vélib bike-share system in Paris, which was run by advertising giant JCDecaux, our SmartBike program had been launched and operated by

A SmartBike from the original Washington, D.C., bike-share program (Daniel Lobo)

Clear Channel, who also contracted with the city to advertise on bus shelters. SmartBike was only one component of a much larger contract. Unfortunately for the city, one line at the end of our agreement outlined the private partner's lackluster commitment to the program. It stated that Clear Channel agreed to set up and operate a bike-share program in Washington, D.C. That's it! Oh no, I thought, this was not terribly sound footing on which to expand our partnership, but let's meet them and see.

In my first meeting with Clear Channel, a few things became clear. They felt that the District had gotten a very rich, fifteen-year deal and associated revenue stream for the bus-shelter contract. They even mentioned that D.C. had "signed the contract at the height of the market." My reaction? "Not really the District's problem." Furthermore, they had recently been purchased by Bain Capital, of Mitt Romney fame, and had little interest in "municipal street furniture," as they saw the program. Lastly, they had no contractual obligation to expand the program, which was true. We were victims of minimal planning for success by government, and an amorphous contract that gave the private sector an easy out. At the end of the day, our incentives were not aligned, and the SmartBike program died as a result. However, this ended up being a blessing in disguise in the long run.

Luckily, Arlington County, Virginia, was planning to launch a bike sharing program around the same time as it became clear that SmartBike's demise was imminent. Because I had a history of partnering with the county, Capital Bikeshare became the first of many projects that we would work on across borders during my tenure. Arlington had already put a procurement process in motion for a bike sharing system and was in the process of receiving bids from vendors. As many jurisdictions do, typically through their regional planning authority, we combined our efforts with Arlington's procurement process to save time and build a regional program. In terms of financing the system, we wanted to use federal money for 80 percent of the cost and applied for Congestion Mitigation Air and Quality funds through the regional metropolitan planning organization. All we needed now was the mayor's agreement to put $1 million into a revamped bike-share program.

My entire conversation with Mayor Fenty about Capital Bikeshare was less than ten minutes. I told him what I wanted to do, and he asked me three simple questions:

- Could our system be the biggest in the United States? Yes.
- Will it be the best? Yes, absolutely.
- Can we minimize the capital D.C. puts in and could it break even or be profitable operationally? I said, "I think so," and aimed to make that happen.

Meanwhile, I had heard about a new bike-share system that had launched in Montreal named Bixi. My wife and I took a vacation to Montreal in our smart car convertible to check it out firsthand, along with the city's heralded new separated bicycle infrastructure. The Bixi system represented a major improvement upon the clunky SmartBike and was modeled on the successful European systems in terms of size and station density. Moreover, the hardware was moveable, rather than SmartBike's fixed stations, and could be installed with a small crane, requiring no capital construction whatsoever. Bixi was also solar powered and required no electrical wiring for its utility. The bikes themselves were solid, streamlined, and modern. They offered a smooth ride and felt more or less bombproof. As a bike industry vet, I could see that they were high quality. As a car-sharing expert, I could see the system's functionality and how well it worked with multiple nodes. When I got back to the United States, I found out that we received only one bid on the procurement, and to my surprise, it was from Bixi, which had partnered with a West Coast planning firm named Alta Planning + Design for the bid. We were a little shocked that there was so little interest, but there was not really an industry yet, and even our existing partner didn't want to make it work. The two companies that partnered on the sole bid were both startups, and were going to need our help and guidance if bike sharing was going to work in the D.C. region, and in the United States.

From the beginning, the bike-share program represented a true collaboration and real public-private partnership. When you are setting up something completely new, at a large scale, there is no room for ego clashes, one-upmanship, or the typical corporate and political wrangling. All five initial partners—the two jurisdictions, our newly shared transportation demand management program (marketing), the manufacturer, and the operator—were aligned in their incentives. We had a goal to launch in one year and there was zero room for error. Why one year? Because neither I nor Arlington had any patience for wasting time, as exhibited by the Zipcar example, and my mayor was running for re-election. What if he didn't win?

Working groups were established as small, cross-functional, and efficient units to manage everything from permitting to public relations and cross-cut D.C. and Arlington. All of our departments, with the exception of engineering, had responsibilities. In D.C., finance, legal, and the CFO's office were all intricately involved in setting up this new operating business. My right hand, Leah Treat, proved instrumental on a number of fronts during this process, including in dealing with the federal government. On top of all this, we had a multi-jurisdictional effort and a complex contract with procurement to hammer out. Scott Kubly, a new hire at DDOT who became my other right hand, had been brought in to run the newly minted "Progressive Transportation Services Administration" a year earlier, which housed Streetcar, the Circulator Bus, and now Capital Bikeshare. Our overarching goal was to launch the system so smoothly, and have our marketing so tight, that people would be shocked that the government ran it.

As we got closer to launch, the consumer-facing aspects of the program became a priority, and being a marketing-focused executive from the private sector, I was hyperfocused on those aspects. As our efforts came to a close, I returned to the basics, the four P's—product, place, promotion, pricing—but the most important P was, of course, the people. The DDOT bike team was doing a lot of the planning and outreach for the system's initial ninety planned stations in D.C. proper. We set up a website and crowdsourced public input about where people wanted bike stations in their D.C. and Arlington neighborhoods. We had just finished rebooting our transportation demand management (TDM)

Launch of Capital Bikeshare (Kevin Kovaleski)

> **A public-private partnership needs to be built on clear expectations, S.M.A.R.T. goals, and a solid contract, but equally important is a healthy, respectful working relationship among all parties.**

program, known as goDCgo, and had again partnered with Arlington County to bring their nationally recognized TDM program to D.C. The new program was essentially top-flight marketing, promotion, and outreach for alternative transportation options. This team was put in charge of coordinating the marketing for the new bicycle transit system.

In keeping with our strong outward communications plan, we partnered with local blogs like the influential and widely read *Greater Greater Washington* and crowdsourced the name for the system, which became Capital Bikeshare. That name organically became "CaBi" for short. The system's website went through multiple iterations until it felt more like a polished private-sector offering such as Zipcar, rather than a stale and opaque city website. I wanted it to be sleek and easy to understand and for the value proposition to stand out and be clear within seconds of loading the site. This became the simple "Join, Take, Ride, Return" that still graces the front page of the system and mirrored Zipcar's

"Join, Reserve, Tap, Return" that we had refined over the years.

By the time we opened the system in September 2010, there was a palpable level of excitement from the public. At our launch event at the U.S. Department of Transportation in Southeast D.C., we brought all the bikes out and had the public sign up to ride them back to stations throughout the city. Throughout the bike share process we had involved the public at every stage, and we wanted them to feel ownership. This was the people's bicycle transit system, CaBi.

We were careful to gradually launch stations for Capital Bikeshare, and later followed the same pattern with Divvy in Chicago. It's crucial for a system to be operationally sound, if not close to flawless, the first time a user tries it. Like any service, you are only as good as the first experience a customer has, and we aimed to learn the rebalancing patterns from day one to avoid empty or full stations as much as possible, which are the bane of the bike-share user experience. Starting with 50 stations in D.C., we ramped up to 110 stations regionally before the end of 2011 when Adrian Fenty left office. The reviews were in and the public loved Capital Bikeshare. Today there are more than 350 stations spanning D.C., Maryland, and Virginia, making it the second largest bike share in the United States by number of stations as of this writing, with more than 10 million trips taken!

Let the public give input on as many aspects of the project as possible.

In D.C., the system broke even on an operations basis (give or take a few thousand dollars) from day one. Keep in mind that this is with zero advertising until 2014 and no sponsorship agreement, two conditions that would be highly unusual today. On top of that it is one of the more expensive systems to run based on it being the first large contract in the United States with no benchmarks on which to base it. How did we pull it off? The user experience was solid. The locals were loyal and signed up in droves. More than 30 percent of initial usage was by tourists and visitors. We had projected single-digit percentage visitor use because SmartBike had no daily use option. The $7 daily user fee subsidized the yearly $75 membership for locals (28 cents per day). Without any advertising at all, the system could foreseeably generate enough profit to fund the 20-percent match needed for capitalization of new equipment for expansion, or replacement of old bikes and stations down the road. With advertising and sponsorship this was virtually assured. Fundamentally though, I credit the relationships among all of the parties involved and the collaboration as being the most important factors in the system's financial stability and success.

Gradually ramp up operations of any large initiative, public or private.

What should you do?

- A public-private partnership needs to be built on clear expectations, S.M.A.R.T. goals, and a solid contract, but equally important is a healthy, respectful working relationship among all parties.
- Align all of your stakeholders' incentives as much as possible, both financially and otherwise. Although Capital Bikeshare may be one of the most "expensive" bike-share systems to operate in the country, the return is also higher. Customer satisfaction and profitability are the envy of other cities. Again, it's not about how much it costs, it's the return on investment that matters.
- Let the public give input on as many aspects of the project as possible.
- Gradually ramp up operations of any large initiative, public or private.
- A focus on profitability drives a better quality of service. Pretty immediately, D.C.'s portion of the Capital Bikeshare system was near breakeven and on its way to making a small profit, with no sponsor or advertising.
- Marketing is critical to success if you have the operations right.

Capital Bikeshare bikes at the launch (Kevin Kovaleski)

Working for the Greater Good

At Bikes USA, Zipcar, and my food-truck company, On The Fly, I learned that doing something positive for people made me feel good. My other interim jobs had left me feeling empty at the end of the day, and disconnected from my fellow human beings; I craved the real, tangible results that I could see manifested daily. For all of us, finding work that we are passionate about is key to our success. It has also been essential in getting results working with or in government, no matter how frustrating that can sometimes be. When you are doing something that customers like and fulfilling a real need, you feel great about it and that comes across in your work and personal life.

Today, governments are striving to enhance their services for the public, and they know that they are often not the best at service delivery. Co-opting the energy of private-sector companies and individuals to do work that is aligned with their goals, beyond profitability, is a critical component of how cities can and will reinvent themselves over the next twenty years. Although I may have seemed like a nontraditional candidate to go into government, and I was, I had built a reputation in D.C. for trying to do good things for the city and taking personal risks to achieve results. That risk-to-reward ratio can be a difficult thing to calculate for each of us, but suffice it to say that nothing great is ever easy to accomplish. If you bring a passion to what you are doing and if there is more to it than money, there's a strong chance that you will be able to bring public and private domains together, and ultimately be successful in your endeavors, often against all odds.

Lesson #7

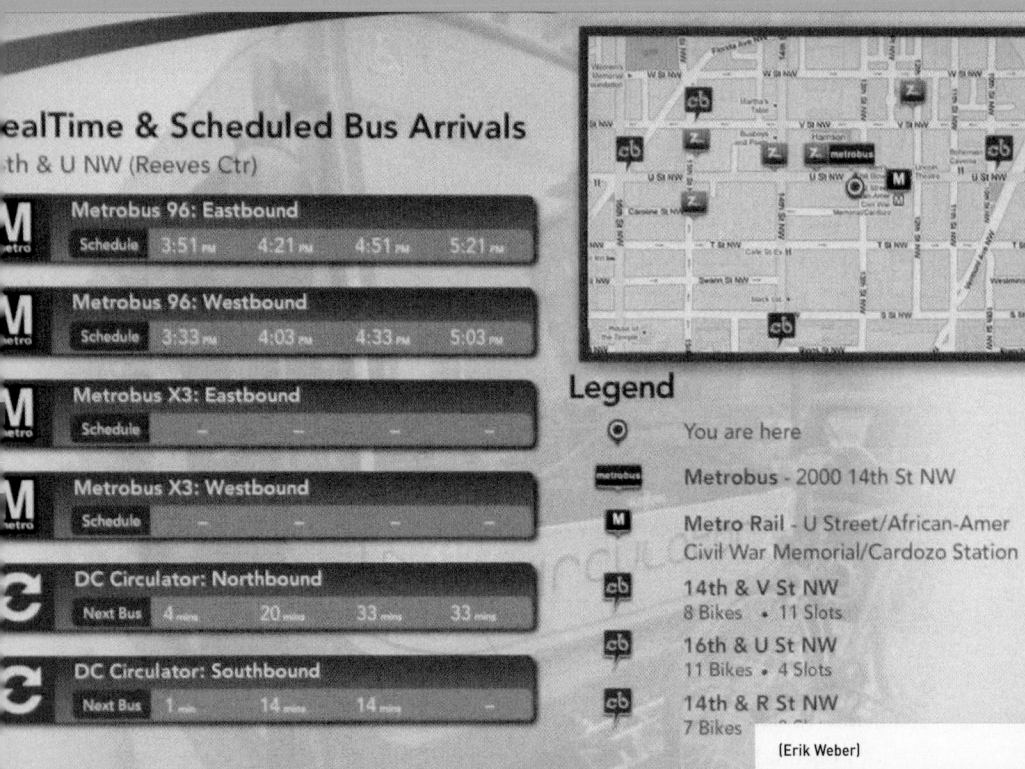

RealTime & Scheduled Bus Arrivals
14th & U NW (Reeves Ctr)

Metrobus 96: Eastbound
Schedule — 3:51 PM — 4:21 PM — 4:51 PM — 5:21 PM

Metrobus 96: Westbound
Schedule — 3:33 PM — 4:03 PM — 4:33 PM — 5:03 PM

Metrobus X3: Eastbound
Schedule — — — — —

Metrobus X3: Westbound
Schedule — — — — —

DC Circulator: Northbound
Next Bus — 4 mins — 20 mins — 33 mins — 33 mins

DC Circulator: Southbound
Next Bus — 1 min — 14 mins — 14 mins — —

Legend

◉ You are here

metrobus — Metrobus - 2000 14th St NW

M — Metro Rail - U Street/African-Amer
Civil War Memorial/Cardozo Station

cb — 14th & V St NW
8 Bikes • 11 Slots

cb — 16th & U St NW
11 Bikes • 4 Slots

cb — 14th & R St NW
7 Bikes •

(Erik Weber)

Metro Bus

36 M6 - Due to

On the present and anticipated technological shifts and business models that are transforming urban life and challenging the status quo

O ver the past decade, smartphones and Internet services have enabled the reinvention of old-line businesses and made them comprehensively more efficient and frictionless for consumers, as well as more profitable. The mobile phone has completely revolutionized our way of life by allowing us to cut the cord, and in the process has generated new business models that are transforming the economy of our cities. In Washington, D.C., for instance, you can now pay for parking via the ParkMobile smartphone application, rather than by putting quarters in a too-often malfunctioning mechanical meter. Residents can apply for any city public-space permit to occupy the curbside using the new TOPS online system, as opposed to spending hours in line in a dreary waiting room. New services such as these offer both cities and their citizens some basic solutions to problems that have long seemed intractable.

Many changes in technology and service delivery have been met with mixed responses by governments, particularly where technology has disrupted an outmoded, overregulated model and made it work better with a fresh

Many changes in technology and service delivery have been met with mixed responses by governments, particularly where technology has disrupted an outmoded, overregulated model and made it work better with a fresh tech-enabled start. Uber's disruption of the taxi industry is the case in point for transportation, while Airbnb represents the foremost current example in the housing and hospitality industries.

tech-enabled start. Uber's disruption of the taxi industry is the case in point for transportation, while Airbnb represents the foremost current example in the housing and hospitality industries. In both cases, technology platforms have capitalized on unmet demand for goods and services by providing access to what I call "lazy assets" (supply) that had latent potential to generate revenue.

It's no accident that the biggest disruptions to date have been in overregulated markets historically stymied by politically powerful but less consumer-oriented industries. Uber and Airbnb, as well as their new-economy competitors, have been buoyed by prevailing cultural trends and the younger generations who balk at a dearth of options in a world increasingly driven by variety and choice. Equally important here is flexibility of price, especially in the large, young, and labor-rich cities such as D.C., San Francisco, and New York. Although many of these companies have either adopted or been subsumed under the label of the "sharing economy," most essentially operate as peer-to-peer platforms that link people (buyers) with those offering services (sellers) at a basic level. Government needs to be ready to adapt to this new paradigm in which many of the old rules based on old models just don't apply. Fundamentally, the peer-to-peer economy is good for cities, and often results in a more sustainable city on a number of levels, so we shouldn't fight the change for the wrong reasons.

One early example of disruption that we take for granted today, but which is actually quite relevant, is that of intercity buses . . .

An early example of disruption: Intercity buses

One early example of disruption that we take for granted today, but which is actually quite relevant, is that of intercity buses, also known in some cities as "Chinatown buses." The Chinatown buses began operating in the late 1990s as an informal service among Chinese immigrants traveling between Boston, New York, Philadelphia, and Washington, D.C. By the late 2000s, it had blossomed into a significant transportation sector with multinational corporate participation.[1] These buses, and their formal competitors, offered convenience and cut-rate pricing, taking advantage of deregulation and curbside pickup (rather than paying bus terminal fees) while paying drivers lower, nonunion wages. Formal new entrants, such as BoltBus and Megabus, though tied to more traditional companies (BoltBus is a joint venture of Greyhound and Peter Pan; Megabus is a division of publicly traded British transportation conglomerate Stagecoach), offered a new slate of services such as Wi-Fi, smartphone ticketing, and more comfortable accommodations for passengers.

In the eyes of many city regulators, the intercity curbside buses were a nuisance. The companies created informal staging areas that blocked sidewalks and created chaotic traffic on the hour. To consumers weary of sloughing their way through dimly lit Greyhound terminals (as well as unguaranteed Greyhound seat tickets that could result in two-hour wait times for the unlucky) or those unable to pay the expensive train fare, these services presented a perfect, intermediate solution for their transportation needs. Around 2010, cities began to craft policy that maintained these services, but relocated them to staging

> In Washington, D.C., we embraced the intercity buses during my tenure at DDOT and, instead of fining them for being rogues, we co-opted them into the formal transportation system, creating city-sanctioned curbside stops for them downtown and ultimately using an underutilized car parking deck to set up an intercity bus terminal at Union Station.

areas where they would pose less of a hazard. In Washington, D.C., we embraced the intercity buses during my tenure at DDOT and, instead of fining them for being rogues, we co-opted them into the formal transportation system, creating city-sanctioned curbside stops for them downtown and ultimately using an underutilized car parking deck to set up an intercity bus terminal at Union Station. Although Amtrak didn't initially like it, we enhanced the city's premier multimodal hub, and given the ever-escalating demand for Amtrak, I think this has probably helped rather than hurt their business.

> ... as we increasingly head toward a "1099 economy," with a greater proportion of city dwellers identifying as "entrepreneurs" or "self-employed" and taking on a variety of roles as independent contractors to make their living, these services provide needed income to fill the gaps.

This pattern of disruption, reactionary regulation, constituency building, and constructive policy-making is hardly a perfect model, but it is a model that will be applied again and again for cities undergoing the change management arising from new business models.

The Taxi Conundrum

On the other side of this coin is the often overlooked supply side ("lazy assets"). Whether you agree with this trend or not, as we increasingly head toward a "1099 economy," with a greater proportion of city dwellers identifying as "entrepreneurs" or "self-employed" and taking on a variety of roles as independent contractors to make their living, these services provide needed income to fill the gaps. When I ride in Lyft cars, for instance, and inquire about how people became Lyft drivers, they typically have multiple jobs or are getting a degree, or they may be starting a business while moonlighting as a Lyft driver. The ability to generate additional income from your largest investments—in your car, your home, or yourself and your education—makes tremendous sense in the information age. Services such as TaskRabbit or HourlyNerd today allow people to use their skills to help those willing to pay for that expertise rather than going to Kelly Services or a consulting firm or through another, more formal process. In real estate, WeWork, Grind, and other coworking facilities have upended the way entrepreneurs think about finding a location to start a business.

So how is this new world affecting the established business constructs we grew up on? What happens to the taxi owners, the phone companies, the building lessors, and the temp services? Well, the answer is that it depends. Every city's regulatory structure and complex market dynamics result in their own characteristics. Let's take taxis, for instance. The Los Angeles taxi market and the D.C. taxi market may seem similar on the face, but in fact, they are diametrically different. Los Angeles has 2,300 licensed taxis in a city of 3.8 million people across 503 sprawling square miles. Washington, D.C., has about 6,500 taxis in a city of 630,000 people over 66 square miles. The land use alone dictates a very different consumer use-pattern for livery services. Los Angeles's taxi business is roughly 85 percent dispatch-driven, meaning that people call their taxis rather than hail them. In Washington, D.C., the opposite is true. D.C. is a hail city; approximately 90 percent of taxi business results from traditional street

> In Washington, D.C., the government and taxi industry have been working together to attempt to create a public-private partnership for 120 taxi companies to operate as one virtual entity with a more flexible regulatory structure.

hails. Los Angeles caps the number of taxis at 2,300, and many of the smaller taxi companies like the cap because they feel that their taxi license is something in limited supply and therefore has value. But, in this new world, another service will come in to meet the demand, and those smaller taxi companies will be proven wrong. In D.C., the system has a looser character and the supply of licenses periodically opens up so that anyone can get one or a fleet owner can add licenses and vehicles to meet demand.

When Uber, Lyft, and others—known as transportation network carriers (TNC)—came along in these two cities, each saw different results. In Los Angeles in early 2015, Uber alone, during ridership peaks, will have more than 5,000 vehicles on the road (and growing), while the taxi industry has remained stuck at 2,300 licenses and has therefore been unable to flex their numbers during peaks to meet demand. In D.C., where the dense environment and the looser regulations have allowed for a more flexible industry, Uber will have 2,000 cars on the road at a given time versus approximately 5,000 licensed taxis. But TNCs are not allowed to, nor is their business model suited to, pick up street hails, which is a big part of the taxi business in Washington. Some D.C. cab companies are having their best year in a decade right now, but the opposite holds true in Los Angeles. So, is Uber destroying the taxi industry or is auto-oriented planning mixed with regressive government regulation driving the outcomes here?

In time, I believe a series of carrots and sticks will be used to encourage and prod both taxi companies and TNCs alike.

The taxi industry in Washington, D.C. proper is valued at around $240 million. Uber alone (not including Lyft) generates approximately $150 million in business for the region. If we assume that two-thirds of their business (or approximately $100 million) falls within the city limits, that means that the overall market has grown by $76 million! Although taxis may be taking a big hit in some markets at the hands of Uber and Lyft, the story is far more nuanced than most have perceived it thus far. One thing is for sure: transportation network companies are growing the ground transportation market, particularly in neighborhoods where people previously did not, or could not, access taxis. I believe that there is strong evidence for this in places such as San Francisco, where the taxi market is $140 million, and the latest numbers for Uber are close to $500 million. In Los Angeles, meanwhile, unless the playing field is leveled from a regulatory standpoint, flexibility is allowed in pricing, and the ceiling on taxi licenses is lifted, the taxi industry will likely not survive in the new world. In Washington, D.C., the government and taxi industry have been working together to attempt to create a public-private partnership for 120 taxi companies to operate as one virtual entity with a more flexible regulatory structure. This cooperative structure allows the industry to set adjustable prices that respond to competition, while also operating under one technology platform and a common marketing scheme that appears cohesive to the public. Within this framework, if successfully implemented, I predict that the taxi industry in D.C. will not only stabilize, but could continue to grow rather than contract in the future.

In time, I believe a series of carrots and sticks will be used to encourage and prod both taxi companies and TNCs alike. These kinds of regulations will encourage taxis to purchase handicapped-accessible vehicles and adopt a citywide application for dispatch across companies, which could benefit both drivers and consumers. Now that the TNCs have proven the validity of the e-hail business, I think taxis, given the right regulatory structure, can take a percentage of that new business. They might even eventually partner with government to provide services such as paratransit, which is a cost center spiraling out of control and threatening the rest of many transit systems' operating budgets. It is critical for both the taxi industry and government to look at the positive outcomes of the TNCs entering the market, understand their strengths, and critically evaluate how they can benefit from their innovations.

Faced with this series of disruptions, city governments have struggled to understand how to effectively regulate these new services, especially when they find themselves wedged between outwardly supportive consumers and the politically savvy unions of ingrained industries. Add to this that government often finds itself on the short end of the financial stick in the Internet business-model world and is thus heavily incentivized to propagate old-line business in which they are ensured a percentage cut, whether from hotel taxes, taxi medallions, or convention fees. For transportation, we have witnessed two typical models of government response:

- The popular cease-and-desist approach, in which regulators either create or default to policy language to ban a particular app or platform (see Haystack example in chapter 6).
- The wait-and-see model, in which regulators and policy makers watch a new business model progress and create a de facto pilot period before either turning to the former strategy or adapting policy to meet the new technology and bend to consumer preferences. Rahm Emanuel did this with the TNCs in Chicago. This has often been accompanied by certain safeguards for the existing industry to survive.

On the private side, companies have adopted one of three approaches:

- They ignore the existing laws and regulatory framework, build a strong constituency and user base to defend themselves (along with enough financial backing to fend off city lawsuits), and launch in spite of policies that restrict their operation, paying fines for their contractors as needed.
- The company works closely with the city to establish a policy or program that fits within the existing legal and regulatory framework of the city, a process that often takes considerable time.
- The company goes to the city, explains its goals, launches, and then works with the city to create a regulatory environment in which it can succeed, even though it may currently operate illegally or outside of the existing paradigm (as Zipcar did).

The Uber Effect

Since 2011, Uber has emerged as the poster child for aggressive, regulation-blind startups in the United States (and increasingly, worldwide). Founded in 2009 as an app to dispatch black cars to pick up passengers with a simple interface that showed you the physical location of the vehicle coming to pick you up, Uber morphed over time into a platform with a wider range of passenger ground transportation options customized to each city's landscape, regulations, and other relevant factors. As they grew, they expanded from black cars to SUVs, then even brought taxis onto the platform as a way to mute backlash from the industry and enter the mainstream, thus lowering the cost of business while taking a $2 matching fee to pair a car with a passenger.

The Uber app

When it came on the scene, Uber completely changed the government/start-up paradigm.

Driving for Lyft, Uber, and Sidecar (Colin@TheTruthAbout on Wikimedia Commons)

When competitor Lyft came on the scene with a platform to pair regular people and their cars with people who needed a lift at much lower cost, Uber quickly copied their business model and added that service to the platform as "uberX" in the United States. Uber's move from a premium service toward the mainstream uberX seems strategically accidental to me, but it worked.

When it came on the scene, Uber completely changed the government/start-up paradigm. Governments were used to being approached and asked for permission to operate a business and then would often take their time figuring out if they wanted to allow it and under what parameters. This could be a long and arduous process for any private-sector company with investors breathing down their neck. I struggled to get government to understand that Zipcar was not "car rental" and that if we tacked on a $9 convention-center surcharge for an $8 hourly rental, then the business didn't work. If the business didn't work, we could not operate and help government to get people out of single-occupancy vehicles, or even better, to sell their car altogether. At Zipcar, we launched and begged for forgiveness too, eventually getting governments from one city to the next to add a "car sharing" business license to their stable, while also recognizing that commercial activities could take place in the driveways of people's homes—a struggle similar to what Airbnb is facing with commercial rental of people's residential spare bedrooms. Unlike Zipcar, which was in some sense taking on the traditional rental car, and was all but ignored by that industry and at first viewed as a nonthreat, Uber is taking on the taxi, which is a tightly government-regulated business in most cities. Because of this and the TNCs' asset-light model, which has allowed for spectacular growth in record time using the assets of private drivers (Zipcar had to buy and lease cars), Uber's growth has resulted in a highly acrimonious battle. Instead of backing off though, Uber has upped the ante and operated illegally if necessary, using public pressure and user support, along with politicians who want to be viewed as innovative, as soldiers in their fight for a $40 billion-plus valuation. It's a pretty brilliant business strategy when you think about it.

I happened to be commissioner of transportation in Chicago when the TNCs started becoming really popular. Mayor Emanuel decided to take a wait-and-see approach and let Uber, Lyft, and Sidecar all operate rather than issuing a cease-and-desist order, as San Francisco and other cities did in 2011. The mayor wanted to let the public decide what worked before deciding upon a regulatory strategy. I endorsed this approach because you can't stifle innovation with an antiquated regulatory framework that existed before the world changed over the last ten to fifteen years. This understandably brought the ire of the taxi companies and the medallion or license owners, who were seeing the value of their assets slip.

The balance of power between government and private companies has shifted definitively over the past few years, and technology has been the driver behind that shift. For instance, government can tell Uber that they can't operate at the airport and pick up passengers, but practically speaking, with unmarked private cars performing the pickup, and smartphones for dispatch and communication, how do you differentiate between Uber and everyday private pick-ups and therefore practically enforce that policy on a day-to-day basis? How does the government enforce a prohibition against Airbnb or VRBO, through which people earn a fee for letting someone stay in their house? Particularly now that people's livelihoods depend on it, this kind of enforcement becomes politically untenable. In reality, any of these centrally transacted platform businesses could be shut down for a variety of reasons—not paying applicable taxes, breaking regulation or established laws, safety concerns, or labor violations. Some or all of these threaten the sharing economy, and some peer-to-peer companies have been shut down, such as LimeWire for file sharing or Aereo for sharing of television and cable signals. In both these cases, the courts shut down these companies after long legal battles. This could happen to Uber if the government decides that Uber's "driver-partners" are actually "driver-employees." This is the risk you take when starting a new business, and Uber is, for better or worse, betting they can make it until the drivers themselves are no longer a factor in their business model.

Toward a new model of public-private collaboration

There is a lot to be excited about right now in cities, in urban planning, and in transportation, from pop-up shops and public spaces, to automated enforcement of traffic laws, protected bike lanes, thriving new public waterfronts, bike sharing, and TNC services, to name just a few. Look at this list and ask yourself what is the common thread. I would argue that none of these advances would be possible without some degree of active public and private collaboration. In some cases, people themselves are taking the public space into their own hands and improving it. Through "tactical urbanism," private citizens have taken it upon themselves to improve public, government-"controlled" spaces by painting their own bike lanes, building community gardens, or painting beautiful murals. In other cases, the government has led the initiative and private companies have followed. Divvy and Capital Bikeshare are prime examples of this approach. In many instances, it has been private companies that take on a leadership role in changing cities. Zipcar and car2go have actively led government toward proactive new policies for car sharing.

More and more, I see government and the private sector playing to their strengths rather than jockeying to control the entire process.

Different cities demand different models and regulations. For instance, the Make Way for People program in Chicago facilitated the creation of innovative public spaces and worked to remove red tape for the special service area (SSA) districts,[2] much like business improvement districts in other cities, to create low-cost public spaces all around the city. CDOT found an innovative way to increase rather than lose parking revenue, crucial in a city where the parking meters were on a 75-year lease to Morgan Stanley, and helped the SSA districts with the site design and the permitting process, as well as community engagement. Business improvement districts have become crucial components of the formula for bridging public and private, often in a hyperlocal context to improve public spaces, development standards, facades, and transportation systems.

In fact, the Make Way for People program was so successful with the SSA districts in Chicago, and so popular with the public, that CDOT put out a request for proposals for a nonprofit to work with private partners to activate all fifty-six plaza spaces that CDOT owned. The plan entailed activating these spaces all around Chicago with public art, local commerce, and digital amenities, including Wi-Fi and screens for information, concerts in Millennium Park, and other public service broadcasting. This program is finally getting under way in 2015 under Luann Hamilton and Janet Attarian's unwavering commitment and leadership at CDOT.

More and more, I see government and the private sector playing to their strengths rather than jockeying to control the entire process. This newfound humility and mutual recognition of strengths and weaknesses is key to any successful public-private collaboration, and to cities continuing to serve as laboratories for innovation, not just in transportation and public space, but in business as well.

Notes

1   For a complete history of the Chinatown bus, see Klein, N., 2009, "Emergent Curbside Intercity Bus Industry: Chinatown and Beyond," Transportation Research Record, *Journal of the Transportation Research Board*, 2111, pp. 83–89.

2   http://www.cityofchicago.org/city/en/depts/dcd/supp_info/special_service_areassaprogram.html/

Lesson #8

Drive Change

Understanding the implications of autonomous, connected mobility, what it means for cities, and how governments can make sure they are driving change, rather than reacting to it

n the beginning of this book, I discussed my reasons for wanting to undertake this work and the imperative for public and private interests to find common ground for the sake of a better future. Much of the discussion that followed has focused on my own personal anecdotes from experience on both sides of this divide. In the last section of the book, I want to shift gears and look forward to talk about the immense changes that are coming, and how you can apply what we have discussed thus far to an unpredictable and fast-moving future. Let's start by looking at what is perhaps the greatest challenge and most exciting innovation that cities will face in the coming decades: the advent of self-driving and connected vehicles.

I believe that over the next ten years and beyond, autonomous and vehicle-to-vehicle technologies will fundamentally change the way we move. These technological shifts will not only transform the public's conception of mobility, but will have profound consequences for the business and government service models that fulfill our transportation needs today.

> **Just as the advent of motorization precipitated a complete reshaping of the city in the early twentieth century, the self-driving car's introduction in cities will be punctuated with moments of painful transition.**

Just as the advent of motorization precipitated a complete reshaping of the city in the early twentieth century, the self-driving car's introduction in cities will be punctuated with moments of painful transition. Many of my peers in the transportation arena, especially those primarily focused on advocating for walking, biking, and transit, express an understandable, reflexive distrust of the self-driving car and similar technologies. Whether stated or not, many find these technologies reflective of a neophilic impulse to blindly upend convention, indulging the futuristic without considering the inherent trade-offs for our quality of life, the built environment, and the economy. Even worse, many of those who are interested in a future of automated, sensor-based technologies are all too willing to draw pedestrians, bicycles, and buses out of their renderings, or forget that the complexity and dynamism of cities relies in part on the unpredictability and serendipitous nature of urban life. As many skeptics see it, a future of "self-driving cars" embodies the rise of a new technocracy, a "solution" to congestion, productivity, and safety issues that is all too quick to forget the many lessons we have learned the hard way by adapting and reshaping our cities around automobiles in the twentieth century.

For these skeptics, I have a plea: Be at the table! Governments, planners, transportation policy makers—people with a sensitivity to the built environment, bicyclists, pedestrians, and transit—need to understand the inherent risks and rewards of this and associated new technologies. We need these skeptics at the table, as I am, so that cities and governments actually anticipate and guide

> **Be at the table! Governments, planners, transportation policy makers—people with a sensitivity to the built environment, bicyclists, pedestrians, and transit—need to understand the inherent risks and rewards of this and associated new technologies.**

this future, rather than only reacting to it, or leaving the policy making to the tech and auto industry behemoths. This is the critical juncture, and for those of us who realize that creating place dwarfs many other concerns in terms of importance, now is the time to pay attention.

Regardless of the potential negatives, I do want to emphasize a lot of the real positives that self-driving vehicles have the potential to bring in the future. For instance, why do we currently accept that it is okay for human beings, who are often distracted, tired, or under the influence of caffeine, alcohol, or prescription drugs, to operate 3,000-pound-plus vehicles in densely populated environments? In the United States and many other places, we have culturally come to accept a large number of fatal "accidents" as the cost of doing business, the cost of "freedom," of driving ourselves. Changing this was the underlying premise of the Vision Zero campaign in Chicago and other cities, and if implemented effectively, may represent one of the most important advances that self-driving vehicles can contribute to society. If we believe that a new technology can reduce, or possibly eliminate traffic deaths, without sacrificing our quality of life, then I think it is our responsibility to explore, foster, and then implement it, within the framework of a responsible set of policies and regulations. We should not accept the status quo or assume that traffic deaths are an insurmountable or inevitable fact of life. We should also not assume that for the implementation of a new technology, we have to sacrifice our overriding ideals in creating beautiful urban places. It will, however, take work to accomplish both.

If we believe that a new technology can reduce, or possibly eliminate traffic deaths, without sacrificing our quality of life, then I think it is our responsibility to explore, foster, and then implement it, within the framework of a responsible set of policies and regulations.

Google self-driving car (Gabe Klein)

Gabe Klein with the Google self-driving car (Sarah Hunter, Google)

One of the most surprising things about how governments perceive technological shifts is that they tend to focus on the long-term consequences, instead of confronting the short-term revolutions happening before their eyes. The earlier that government agencies can grasp how quickly businesses such as Uber will flex their business models and transform into automated vehicle technology companies, the faster that governments can begin to prioritize the needs that they value in a policy framework.

Of course, the truth is that many autonomous features are already available in vehicles today, and have been incrementally introduced into vehicles since the 1970s. Ford, Volvo, Nissan, and other companies have recently built collision avoidance systems that can adjust vehicle speed and position based on cameras or sensors picking up changes in the right-of-way. This incremental introduction of the autonomous technologies foreshadows the larger technological shift on the cusp of taking hold. For instance, Elon Musk, chief product architect and cofounder of Tesla Motors, has stated publicly that by 2015 he wants to have a "Level 3" autonomous car in which you can turn the autonomous features on and off voluntarily (he originally set the potential launch for 2017). There are pros and cons to this type of system. Some feel that drivers could be lulled into a false sense of security and forget that they turned it off, or become confused between the on and off modes, resulting in more accidents. However, this is where policy comes into play, and there are other considerations that could be positive.

Cities could require vehicles to drive in an autonomous mode within city limits, or on local streets with thirty-five mile per hour or lower speed limits.

Signage can communicate these zone-based requirements to the vehicle directly via cameras, indicating that a car must enter into autonomous mode, the next generation of what speed cameras and congestion-charging schemes do today. Vehicle manufacturers can create features that will pull a car over and shut it off if a driver does not obey the law, is clearly under the influence of a substance, or is driving recklessly due to distraction.

Will the regulations catch up to allow fully autonomous driving? Will it take twenty years for this technology to actually take hold on city streets? Over the following pages, I want to share my own insights and projections on this topic. These ideas are based on discussions with my contacts in technology companies, auto companies, government, and the policy arena, as well as how I believe the public and private sector might interact and collaborate going forward.

For any discussion of autonomous vehicles, it is critical to first understand some of the nuances and different types of technologies that tend to be subsumed under the same umbrella. Specifically, when most people talk about autonomy, they are often referring to two separate but related technological trends: vehicle-to-vehicle technology (V2V) and self-driving/autonomous cars.

V2V, or the dynamic wireless exchange of data between active, moving vehicles, has been supported by U.S. DOT research grants for years. V2V is based on creating a technological ecosystem in which vehicles in close range are in constant communication with one another, greatly enhancing both the safety and efficiency of roadways. The federal government has invested considerable resources into V2V and vehicle-to-infrastructure (V2I) research and

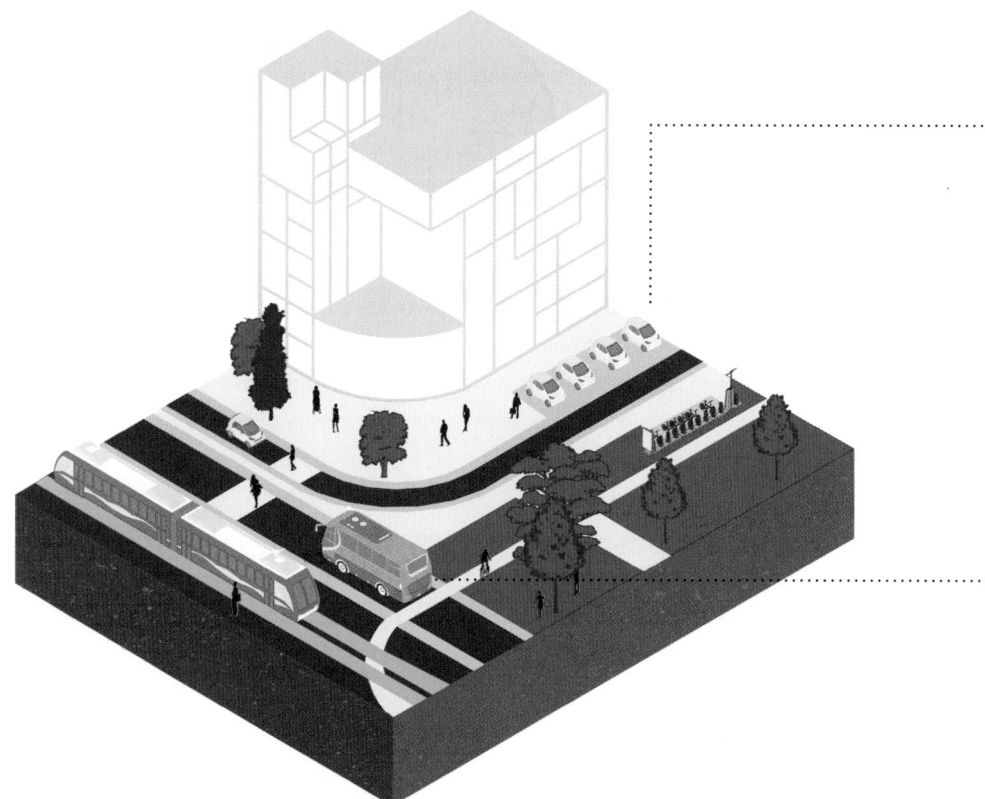

Autonomous Futures

The Evolution of a New Paradigm for Autonomous and Connected Mobility

Electric, light-weight urban vehicles

On-demand, subscription services

Self-driving vehicles running slowly in convoys on shared streets

Autonomous on-demand transit

Expanded transit backbone

Bike-sharing connectivity, separated facilities on larger streets, greenway networks linking our towns

A new framework for safer cities is emerging based on trends in sensor technology, changing lifestyles, and mobile connectivity.

Cities of the future can leverage the benefits of autonomous technology for an achievable and true Vision Zero, to reclaim public space for people and active transportation, extend the transit backbone, and to provide new transportation options and equity where it is lacking today.

Autonomous future (infographic by Kate Chanba and David Vega-Barachowitz)

standards for a multitude of reasons, including maximizing the efficiency of existing roadways, congestion mitigation, and most important, safety. Many believe that vehicle-to-infrastructure would require substantial capital investments by governments for communicative technologies embedded in roadways and other infrastructure and systems. V2V is viewed as more realistic for quick implementation in the United States because private auto companies can simply build this technology into future models, based on federal guidelines. In fact, the U.S. DOT will be requiring V2V features on all vehicles in the not too distant future. V2I systems, on the other hand, rely on expenditures by the federal government on public assets, and could therefore take decades to scale. As a result, industry standards are being formulated so that a Volvo can talk to a Ford, for instance. V2V technology, when paired with autonomous driving, will ultimately allow vehicles of all types to essentially run in automated convoys, like a train set, but on the road.

Most of the self-driving or autonomous vehicle technologies rely on a careful mapping of the existing street network, which is constantly enhanced by learned behavior. These systems then employ various cameras, radar, and sensor-based mechanisms to be responsive to environmental cues and errors by other users, and to continue to gather data on learned behavior. Autonomous vehicle technology exists in cars today, but most people don't think of it in those terms. Basic cruise control has been a staple since the 1980s. Modern, adaptive semi-automation, meanwhile, has created the ability for lasers and sensors to automatically brake vehicles or to dynamically adjust to posted speed limits or traffic calming cues, both of which are configured in a database of the mapping system.

The different levels of autonomous vehicles are explained below.

Levels of Autonomous Vehicles (National Highway Transportation Safety Administration, 2013)

- **Level 1**—Function-specific automation: Automation of specific control functions, such as cruise control, lane guidance, and automated parallel parking. Drivers are fully engaged and responsible for overall vehicle control (hands on the steering wheel and foot on the pedal at all times).
- **Level 2**—Combined function automation: Automation of multiple and integrated control functions, such as adaptive cruise control with lane centering. Drivers are responsible for monitoring the roadway and are expected to be available for control at all times, but under certain conditions can be disengaged from vehicle operation (hands off the steering wheel and foot off pedal simultaneously).
- **Level 3**—Limited self-driving automation: Drivers can cede all safety-critical functions under certain conditions and rely on the vehicle to monitor for changes in those conditions that will require transition back to driver control. Drivers are not expected to constantly monitor the roadway.
- **Level 4**—Full self-driving automation: Vehicles can perform all driving functions and monitor roadway conditions for an entire trip, and so may operate with occupants who cannot drive and without human occupants.

Given this technology spectrum, it is critical to understand how Silicon Valley tech companies are approaching autonomous vehicles, in contrast to the big Detroit and European automakers. Google and Apple actually see the technology as an extension of their operating platforms and an evolution of mobile connectivity into a service for getting people around. The automakers, meanwhile, do not want to be tethered to these tech behemoths, even for mapping software, never mind the entire technology platform that will power their cars. (Hint: Have you ever wondered why the mapping software in your car is so terrible? Because they don't want to use Google maps!) Today's biggest disruptor in the arena, Uber, has turned everything

> **It takes Ford or GM seven years on average to take one new vehicle from the drawing board to dealerships. Although the tech companies have their own issues, many stemming from their relative isolation on campuses in the suburbs, they have the advantage of being design-driven, particularly at Apple, and curiosity-driven, particularly at Google. Moreover, they are not afraid to experiment or challenge the status quo.**

upside down by forcing their way in the door and building a $40-billion company in the blink of an eye. Uber has demonstrated to the automotive and technology industries that ground transportation as a service may potentially be a bigger business than anyone realized. As a result, the extensions of that business from the hardware to software to advertising are more up for grabs in an automated world than any of these players had realized, and sooner than most had predicted.

Uber and Lyft have done the hard work of gaining acceptance for the new service paradigm, which meshes well with the autonomous urban future that Google envisions, replete with shared-use robo-cabs. But the automakers have generally been testing a different type of self-driving vehicle: the kind that is big, bulky, and drives on the highway from the suburbs to the city and back. They are betting, for the most part, that a large segment of the public will continue to purchase cars and fit them into the same land use patterns that we have developed since the 1950s. And why not? Their entire business model depends on it, and undoing land use errors is a costly, revolutionary enterprise. GM, Toyota, and a few others have been testing ultrasmall personal mobility vehicles for urban use, but as a secondary pursuit, as opposed to a primary effort.

So which of these actors will prevail? The auto giants tend to be engineer-driven. As I learned firsthand at DDOT and then in Chicago, an engineer-driven organization can be difficult to move quickly. I have heard the same from auto companies that are themselves working to innovate. Engineers are, by and large, methodical, process-oriented, and precise to the point of being somewhat conservative. It takes Ford or GM seven years on average to take one new vehicle from the drawing board to dealerships. Although the tech companies have their own issues, many stemming from their relative isolation on campuses in the suburbs, they have the advantage of being design-driven, particularly at Apple, and curiosity-driven, particularly at Google. Moreover, they are not afraid to experiment or challenge the status quo. Although it is true that the auto companies have established experimental labs and think tanks that are gradually changing this, such as Ford's Silicon Valley lab, they remain largely engineer-driven bureaucracies that run more like government agencies than nimble startups. At Facebook, for example, anyone can walk up to Mark Zuckerberg anytime and pitch him on an idea. He works in a glass room and is frequently sitting out in the courtyard talking to employees. It's a completely different world than Detroit.

Bloomingdale Trail (Framework design team: Arup, Ross Barney Architects, Michael Van Valkenburgh Associates, Chicago Public Art Group)

From a business perspective, tech companies see autonomous cars as a service-driven business opportunity, not to mention a trove of data for the platforms that run them. They have no interest in ultimately becoming manufacturing giants. Google partners with handset and computer makers to build its hardware, while they provide the platform. Apple outsources to manufacturers such as Foxconn in China to build their hardware, supplies the iOS operating system, and sells the package. They both use third-party telecommunications networks. Daimler, Ford, and BMW, on the other hand, are all manufacturers, with designers, engineers, and mini technology companies in-house. It's likely that these two worlds will need each other and may even form partnerships in the future.

However, for self-driving cars, the "Big 3" auto companies (Ford, GM, and Chrysler) no longer control the landscape or garner such clout that the Silicon Valley entrepreneurs have to work with them. The auto industry has become far more global, with companies such as Volkswagen, Daimler, and BMW in Germany, Tata in India, Tesla in the United States, and new, innovative vehicle manufacturers such as Cherry in China popping up left and right to address huge new markets. The slow-moving behemoths in the auto manufacturing industry will experience significant upheaval in a world where urban vehicle complexity, individual car ownership, and in turn, the total market size will all shrink. Ultimately, it is the pace of innovation and the culture of change in the start-up and technology companies that will be toughest to reckon with. Ten years ago, there were almost no smartphones and neither Uber nor Lyft.

> **The most significant opportunity for a future of driverless vehicles beyond pure safety, at least from the progressive urbanist's point of view, is that cities will have the opportunity to reclaim a lot of land currently devoted to automobiles and their storage.**

Imagine where things will be ten years from now. What we are witnessing today is a battle for the future of our ground transportation systems. In the face of this battle, the people and their governments need to set the right framework for these technologies to hit the ground in favor of people rather than just profit, not losing sight of many of the positive ideals and constructs that we value about city life.

So how can we prepare our cities for these changes without knowing exactly how this future will begin to take shape and how fast mass adoption will take hold? I want to offer some ideas for policy makers on how these technologies might be framed as a vehicle to achieve other policy goals. For those who already believe in a self-driving future, these ideas are meant to expand your conception of how this technology can achieve positive social goals and ideals.

The most significant opportunity for a future of driverless vehicles beyond pure safety, at least from the progressive urbanist's point of view, is that cities will have the opportunity to reclaim a lot of land currently devoted to automobiles and their storage. In most of the discussions around self-driving cars, the big opportunity to create better cities and public spaces often gets lost. The inevitable inefficiencies of the personal automobile have resulted in twentieth-century cities of asphalt and parking lots. Sixty percent of Los Angeles is devoted to private parking lots, and many other cities are in the 40–60-percent range. Driverless, connected cars will be able to use one narrow travel lane much more efficiently, and once perfected, may obviate the need for excessive turn lanes, signals, and ultimately, vehicle storage. Many streets, particularly low-volume roads, can be built for light electric vehicles running on parallel tracks, rather than engineered to sustain the weight of a freight truck. Decades from now, when all vehicles are autonomous in urban centers, traffic signalization may become a thing of the past, and pedestrians should ultimately have priority and attain more freedom of movement. If the right framework is put in place (and that's a big if), self-driving vehicles can help justify the eradication of parking minimums in developments and dramatically cut on-street parking, possibly up to 85 percent if forecasts for shared mobility are accurate in an autonomous world. We can even better make the case for pedestrian-only or pedestrian-priority shared streets (though there's no excuse for not doing more of this now). Parking spaces can give way to on-street shared-use paths, or "slow lanes," that encourage shared use by any mode that wants to travel below fifteen miles per hour and weighs less than, say, five hundred pounds. I can even imagine a scenario in which streets are designed as large, pervious surfaces that are not only more beautiful, breaking down barriers between sidewalks and roads, but can also help our cities become more resilient.

Vehicles today are only in use approximately 5 percent of the time.[1] The rest of the day, they take up valuable space that could be put toward other public uses. That's a big sacrifice we've made, and I think that self-driving cars are part of our opportunity to fix it. As mobility evolves from a private luxury into a subscription service in the "internet of everything" world, vehicles (in urban areas, at least) can be active 95 percent of the time while serving multiple customers rather than sitting around unused 95 percent of the time. As a result, societies will not need anywhere near as many vehicles as we have today. In the United States, we have 300 million people and 250 million vehicles.[2] In China, they have 1.3 billion people and 100 million vehicles. Can autonomous vehicles and new service models save us from further damaging the planet by stemming the tide of vehicle ownership in emerging middle class economies? In the United States alone, the Intelligent Transportation Society of America estimated a 2–4-percent reduction of Americans' fossil fuel use, each year, for the next ten years as these technologies begin to take hold.

The critical case for the self-driving car lies in the domain of safety. As I have mentioned before, and Vision Zero campaigns all across the country are

1   Shoup, D., *The High Cost of Free Parking, Updated Edition* (Chicago: Planners Press), chapter 1.

2   http://www.greencarreports.com/news/1093560_1-2-billion-vehicles-on-worlds-roads-now-2-billion-by-2035-report

Along with safety, the accessibility of the autonomous vehicle to those with disabilities, the elderly, and even children, has the potential to be an enormously positive step in our society, both in terms of access and equity.

finally helping us realize, no traffic fatality should be treated as an acceptable byproduct of automobility. Today, more than 90 percent of road crashes are caused by driver error. Google and other companies working on this technology are making safety a central part of their appeal to city and state regulators, and governments know that this is an intractable problem that safety campaigns and street improvements alone may not solve. That said, I think it's critical to emphasize that safety should not be used as the sole justification for self-driving vehicles. Traffic engineers often use "safety" as a defense when they widen roads or remove crosswalks on busy roads. Pedestrian overpasses and underpasses, which can compromise personal safety in other ways, are often justified using the same logic. So we need to contextualize the public safety and public health benefits of driverless vehicles in terms of how they contribute to a better quality of life. In this way, we can push ourselves toward a better result, and ultimately, a better future. It is critical that we do not place pedestrians and other active users of the streets in the background in the interest of free-flowing autonomous pods and zero congestion. Although we might reduce deaths to nearly zero, we would have missed the opportunity to create a place where people actually want to live, and where human activity is the priority rather than a marginal activity, as it already is today in many places as a result of our ingrained car culture and the policies that endorse it.

Along with safety, the accessibility of the autonomous vehicle to those with disabilities, the elderly, and even children, has the potential to be an enormously positive step in our society, both in terms of access and equity. That said, although this has been a major rallying point for many companies working on the technology, there has been very little discussion of accessibility as it compares to price. For instance, how can self-driving vehicle service delivery models dovetail with or ultimately replace paratransit and similar services in an affordable way that does not exacerbate existing inequalities? Equity could represent a major blind spot if not made a central tenet of the conversation instead of a sidebar. It rests in the hands of governments to not only understand the technological and operational potential of self-driving vehicles, but to create an equitable framework in which they can operate. I believe we can, and I want to see governments collaborate with social entrepreneurs in the private sector to foster innovative business models so that self-driving cars can actually be used as a tool to increase access and equitability, along with safety. If this tack is not taken, there is a risk that these services left solely to the free market could instead reinforce existing stratifications, undermining public transit systems and making mobility even more of a luxury good.

Policy makers need to be thinking about these risks and creating the safeguards to ensure that driving becomes a more public, shared, common good as opposed to a private, individual, luxury one. With the potential to lower costs of vehicles, labor, and fuel, and layering on shared rides and transportation as a service, not only should costs go down dramatically, but utilization could rise by a factor of nineteen (because vehicles could be in use 95 percent of the time as opposed to 5 percent of the time). The resulting economies could be very equitable if the public sector simply begins by learning, engaging, and guiding the change now. There has been very little discussion of this to date, and it represents one of the biggest opportunities for forward-looking transportation policy makers to begin making a mark.

So what is the role of public transit in all of this and how can we enhance transit in a future of driverless cars? In my opinion, high-quality, high-speed services that move large volumes of people during peak times are here to stay. Subway, light rail, streetcars, bus rapid transit, and many high-volume regional and local buses are likely going to be here in perpetuity, and I think these services can grow dramatically over time, in keeping with many of the land use, lifestyle, and cultural trends that we are already seeing. But lower quality services, such as unreliable local bus networks and mediocre suburban and rural transit, are ripe for disruption in this new world. Fundamentally this is because these services are extremely expensive on a per-ride basis and do not serve customers especially well in terms of frequency, speed, and overall experience. From the progressive urbanist's perspective today, we tend to think bus = good and car = bad. This is based on single-occupancy personal vehicles versus city buses running at close to full capacity. When you have two to four people per shared Toyota Prius instead of a city bus that is less than half full and gets four miles per gallon, the reality starts to look a lot different.

In the future, we need to calculate the actual efficiency of these vehicles per person, per mile, including the environmental impacts. In a world of autonomous vehicles, a car with three to four passengers is going to win in terms of efficiency, comfort, end-to-end connectivity, and trip time in most cases. This should make transit managers and planners uncomfortable, but it is a reality that they should confront now in anticipation of reinventing their own models and adapting them to the advent of these new technologies. They should be co-opting autonomous technology into their own services and into planning for multimodal connectivity, and strive to understand how these vehicles can serve as feeders to the transit backbone in the future.

In the long term, transit systems need to completely change their approach to customer service, multimodality, open data, payment systems, and network

> ... high-quality, fixed-route transit
> can't and won't go away ...

building. Otherwise, these agencies risk irrelevance beyond running the backbone of the system. Today many of the older, more-established agencies see themselves as "operators" and focus on the nuts and bolts of running the system day to day, while struggling to finance their aging infrastructure, physically maintain it, and deal with the unions for their large labor pools. This leaves innovation around the business model and a focus on the customer as an afterthought in many cases, which is very unfortunate. To become more nimble, flexible, and customer-oriented, many of these agencies should contract out service to private operators that are completely focused on operating transit at a 99.99997-percent service level, and have continuous process improvement and other management systems in place. The transit agency can then free up time to focus on serving the end user with a suite of offerings that they coordinate and that reinforce one another, such as transit-oriented development and the associated value capture strategies, car sharing, ride sharing, bike sharing, subway, streetcar, carpool, real-time information, way finding, and marketing.

If transit agencies do not step up, free up, and transform, then carpool, ride share, and flexible jitney services will begin to eat up a larger swath of tomorrow's transit business as we urbanize. There is actually a tremendous amount of profit to be made by a transit agency and I, for one, see no reason that an agency cannot be profitable from an operations standpoint if it outsources some functions and leverages the immense assets at its disposal, particularly land around the transit backbone. Hong Kong's transit system is also a land development company, and makes money from the transit-oriented development that it creates, thereby funding transit operations. Chris Leinberger and colleagues, along with Smart Growth America, published a study in 2015 on the City of Boston and the importance of walk-ups and walkability, showing that 6 percent of the land in the city houses 37 percent of the real estate footage, 40 percent of the population, and 42 percent of employment opportunities, all around transit nodes in walkable communities.[3] This demonstrates why high-quality, fixed-route transit can't and won't go away, but also why transit agencies need to reinvent themselves so that they can take advantage of the land use–transit nexus. Beyond real estate, I am convinced that the multijurisdictional governments responsible for the governance of these often regional systems need to play a much bigger role in an autonomous future, if they can reorganize themselves to do so productively.

Transportation network companies such as Lyft, taxis, private bus services, and even FedEx are all, to some extent, positioning themselves to morph into ground transportation network platforms. Car companies are actively getting into the service business. Daimler is one great example of this and has ten-plus service companies, including car2go and RideScout, a multimodal aggregator application that I advised until their purchase by Daimler in 2014. Ford has announced twenty-five mobility pilots that will incubate new business services, including flexible bus service in London and New York and car sharing in India. BMW has launched DriveNow car sharing as a joint venture

3   Leinberger, C., P. Lynch, and the George Washington University School of Business, *The WalkUP Wake-up Call: Boston*, Smart Growth America, March 2015. http://www.smartgrowthamerica.org/tag/walkups/

with Sixt rental car and invested in on-demand valet service. At the same time, Uber has announced that they are working on their own vehicle with Carnegie Mellon University.

So where are we headed? I think that there could be significant consolidation between new and old companies over time. Could Uber merge with a GM or BMW? Could Lyft be purchased by Apple? There are many possibilities and configurations, and what scares these companies, new and old, is how fast an upstart could disrupt them all. Each one wants to be the Amazon of urban transportation. The next best thing is to accumulate a large valuation so that said company can buy their upstart competition, as Facebook did with Instagram.

Tesla, of course, is the wild card in much of this—an unusual company with an enigmatic founder who is himself an engineer, a software expert, a successful payment services entrepreneur, an auto manufacturer, the largest solar provider in the United States, and a space pioneer. That's an impressive resume for a forty-three-year-old. Elon Musk bought a Toyota factory for mass production of the current, expensive Tesla Model S and the future Model X that is planned to come in at around a $30,000 price point. Musk is rumored to be considering partnering with Apple on their iCar, which I imagine would be city-focused, like the Google car, rather than the more conventional auto focus and scale that Tesla has undertaken to date.

In some ways, Tesla represents the only bridge between the new tech industry and the old auto manufacturing industry, at least in the United States. Tesla may answer the question of who will build the urban mobility vehicles of the future, and whether they will run on a specific platform. Their speculative valuation is higher than many traditional auto companies, and they have the resources to create a new vehicle segment without being burdened by the culture or bureaucracy of the traditional auto companies. Best of all, they are not afraid to fail, which is key to pushing the envelope and succeeding.

Looking forward, I think that government needs to understand, and in many ways embrace, the realities that are emerging around them rather than propping up models that may be outmoded and fiefdoms that have no significance to the average consumer. I learned on the inside that changing government is not easy, and there are many stakeholders at play here, including taxi commissions, bus drivers' unions, and traditional auto and energy companies, whose years may ultimately be numbered. Governments need to understand that in the new world, there may be much more power in the soft side, such as regulations, contracts, marketing channels, and oversight, than the hard side of the equation, such as buying buses and having employees physically operating services. The government will play a larger role in creating the incentives around which private actors operate rather than being a service provider, and this could be a big win for everyone.

So how can governments actually act on what's important and fulfill their mission for the public? And what is the recipe for the responsible deployment of these technologies over the next five to fifteen years? To start with, I think that governments, planners, and sustainable transportation advocates need to be in the room. Rather than just focusing on the regulations and the legal side of the equation, policy makers and advocates for biking, walking, transit, and public spaces need to be at the forefront of understanding (1) what kinds of infrastructural adaptations would actually be required to adapt the environment for these technologies, (2) the inherent trade-offs to the different potential outcomes, and (3) how to focus on the positives of self-driving cars, such as increased space and safety for people, while using the technology as a means to disincentivize car ownership, wasteful driving, and poor land use decisions.

In other words, we need to create the design guidelines of the future today and craft a comprehensive vision that is actually less about driverless cars and smart cities, and more about the reclamation of the public realm, the democratization of mobility, and a shift toward focusing on quality of life rather than time saving and efficiency alone. If governments don't get their priorities straight and get this right, we will recreate existing stratifications and render people out of the canvas that is the future city. I've seen too many images of self-driving cars in which every one of the passengers is working on a laptop or on the phone. Doesn't that miss the point? The real innovation here begins at a convergence of old and new, by restaging the things that matter most—playing board games with family members, biking with your friends, crossing Main Street without taking your life in your hands—through the advent of a new technology. We must make sure that innovation for the sake of innovation doesn't become the focal point and that we don't lose the forest for the trees. Technology is merely a means to an end—in this case a means to help achieve the quality of life that people of all walks of life deserve on the streets that we call home.

Conclusion

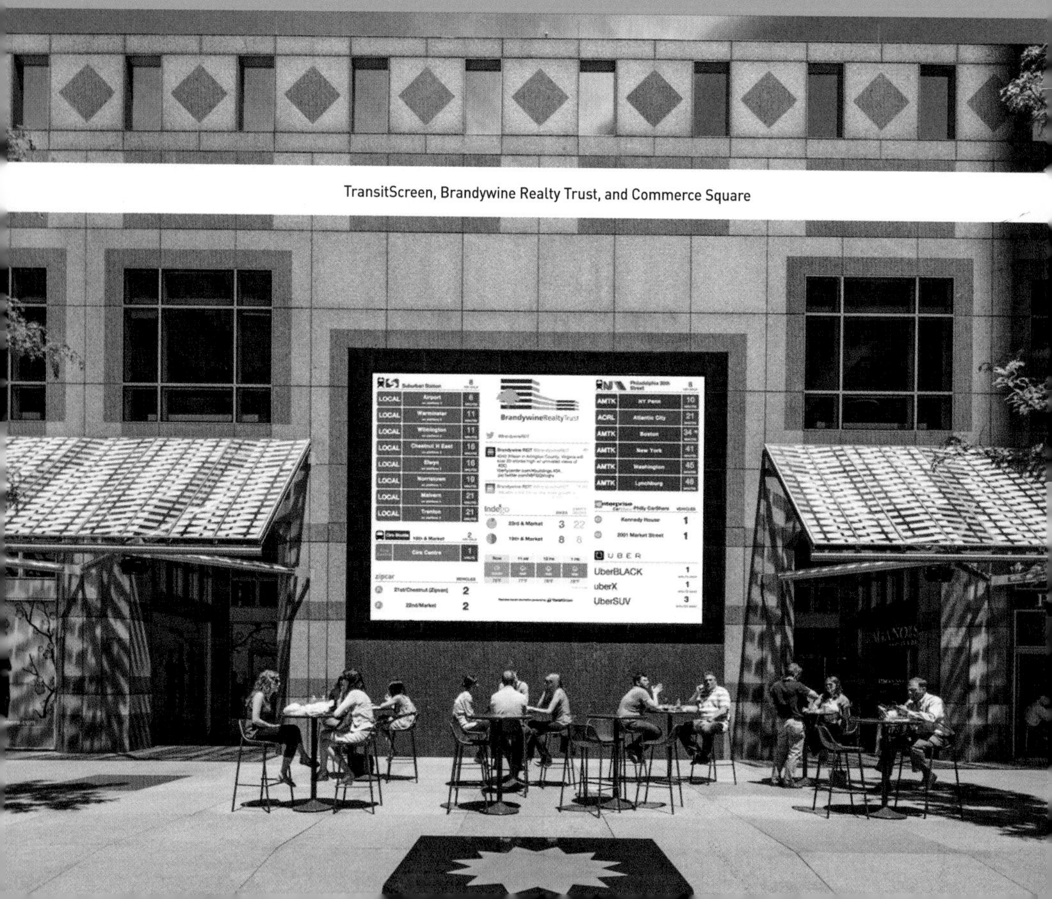

TransitScreen, Brandywine Realty Trust, and Commerce Square

The Big Picture and You

The stories contained in this book are linked by certain common themes: public and private social entrepreneurship, progressive management, and public-private collaboration, to name just a few. But how can these principles, and the lessons contained therein, be translated into practice or overlaid onto future scenarios and future disruptions in cities? The answer, in my mind, is that the rate of change occurring in today's technology-rich environment demands unprecedented, fast action if entities and leaders are going to remain relevant. Government leaders in particular have to transform themselves and their policy-setting apparatus if they want to play a relevant role in shaping change. If they succeed, we will be in a much better position for the public and private sectors to collaboratively foster better lives in our cities.

I want to end this book with a broad discussion of the greatest challenges and opportunities that cities could face in the coming decades, and how we can seize these opportunities, quickly, to shape the cities we want. I would also like to speculate, perhaps somewhat optimistically, about how many of the trends I have discussed will manifest themselves in cities five to twenty-five years in the future.

In conceiving this future, I want to stress how important it is to see the implications of such changes beyond transportation alone. Whether we are

> **How we configure our future neighborhoods and transportation systems will have profound impacts on climate change, on socioeconomic mobility, and on public health. The ground is shifting beneath us, and whether you're talking about energy or health-care or climate, the landscape is evolving more quickly than we can even begin to anticipate.**

analyzing it through a historical lens or projecting into the future, transportation goes well beyond the simple act of moving from A to B at X speed. Many of the transportation challenges we see today can overwhelmingly be attributed to land use planning and engineering mistakes made in America throughout the twentieth century, and then exported to countries around the world. Those decisions have dislocated our workplaces and daily routines from our neighborhoods and home lives. Our transportation systems and public spaces have, over time, come to reflect our societal values and aspirations, and in many ways, both embody and then shape those values for future generations.

The future challenges and opportunities we face in cities are not just about the obvious—the advent of high-tech vehicles, apps, or even traditional transportation. How we configure our future neighborhoods and transportation systems will have profound impacts on climate change, on socioeconomic mobility, and on public health. The ground is shifting beneath us, and whether you're talking about energy or healthcare or climate, the landscape is evolving more quickly than we can even begin to anticipate. This is why our North Star cannot be about technology for the sake of technology alone. Instead, we must use the momentum of technological change as a force to help us create places that celebrate public life.

When predicting the changes that we will witness in cities, we need to put technological change within the context of massive population growth, climate change, and unchecked resource depletion. These are not presuppositions at this point, it's just a matter of how much and how fast. So, if we feel pretty sure of our assumptions about urbanization—that 2 billion more people will occupy the planet by 2050—then we need to look holistically at what cities and their systems will look like by 2020, by 2040, and beyond. Of course, there are many things we don't know, and innovations and new business models we're not yet aware of, from biosynthesis to virtual reality and holographic imaging to three-dimensional (3-D) printing, food printing, and artificial intelligence. All of these innovations will have profound effects on how people live, work, and play in the future, as well as the amount of time that we spend on these activities. Although this adds to uncertainty, it should also make us hopeful that we not only have the ability to change, fast, but that human ingenuity layered onto raw computing power can produce some remarkable advancements that are key to a bright future.

Looking at technological trends in some major areas of potential disruption—renewable energy, urban aquaponic and vertical food production, local 3-D printing of products, online education, or automation of today's more mundane human jobs and tasks—there are a few common threads. We see a continued trend toward dramatically increased efficiency, decentralized production, and smaller carbon footprints. These topics likely deserve their own books, or at least chapters, but let us think broadly for a moment. Together, these trends have the potential to decentralize production of goods, food, and energy, allowing for less travel and more local investment, and even perhaps greater self-sufficiency.

So what might our lives look like in 2030? 2050? Having listened and talked to a lot of futurists, economists, theorists, and urbanists, I believe that we will lead very different lives day to day, and they may be more fulfilling and fun. The production of many "things" will likely decentralize to our homes and communities through the 3-D printing of cloud-based technical schematics that rely on locally produced raw materials. Humans will no longer drive cars in cities, making all forms of transportation safer, particularly walking and biking, which will be allotted more space on our streets. This will forever change our car culture by desexualizing the automobile as it evolves into a utilitarian pod with technology interfaces, at least in dense urban areas. Energy, meanwhile, will shift from today's traditional utility-driven model with central production and distribution to predominantly decentralized renewable energy production, especially solar and wind power, at the point of usage. Batteries will allow storage off-peak and the ability to meet demand at peak through a peer-to-peer electrical grid in each neighborhood. This will lower our energy costs to close to zero and forever upend entrenched industries, many of whom have been largely responsible for climate change. Much of our long-haul business travel may ultimately be replaced by e-meetings that use virtual reality and holographic technology. These technologies can place us in a conference room or on a stage seamlessly, even while we sit on our couch with only a headset or Internet-enabled contact lenses on.

It's easy to see the future as an overwhelming technological ecosystem, as complex and unwieldy as it is incomprehensible. I'm not going to say that this is not a possible outcome, particularly if we don't get a handle on issues such as climate change, but I see a potentially different picture—a simpler life.

How can I make these predictions so assuredly? Because nascent versions of these innovations are already rapidly taking hold, and many are on the cusp of becoming integral to our daily lives. For example, in energy, which is crucial to transportation efficiency and mitigating climate change more broadly, we are seeing greater investment in renewable energies than the traditional fossil fuels industry. The International Energy Agency now estimates that solar will be the largest single source of energy by 2050. Norway and its Sovereign Wealth Fund just announced a $900 billion divestiture from fossil fuel investments. These are huge bellwethers for the future.

As our economy goes from industrial and postindustrial to the information age, jobs as we know them today will evolve as automation replaces the most mundane tasks and even some advanced work. We have already seen the part-time worker population double over the last ten years as the "1099 economy" ramps up with equal parts benefit and detriment thus far by most counts.

If our energy costs are lowered (or even free?) because energy is self-generated and renewable, if ground transportation costs drop dramatically via autonomous and vehicle-to-vehicle technologies combined with shared-use models, if the consumer products that we buy are significantly lower-cost due to 3-D printing and recycling, if we can travel anywhere virtually and on-demand,

Some of the questions I am leaving you with don't have easy answers. But just because there is uncertainty does not mean that there is not a road map for managing and shaping the future.

and if computers are automating the mundane tasks of our lives, and citywide free Wi-Fi is ubiquitous, then how much money do we really need? The answer is not as much, and potentially dramatically less. We need a roof over our heads first and foremost, and of course food and water. Beyond that? It will be a matter of luxuries. In this new paradigm, "things" will not necessarily have an assigned "cost" to them and may be bartered freely or shared in communities once the ownership model falls away and traditional manufacturing becomes individualized. The things that we prize today will then have less intrinsic value and will likely not define people as a result. This redefinition of the importance of wealth and stuff is a big opportunity in striving toward economic equality.

If we add up all of the changes outlined in this book, primarily on our streets and related to how we move, but also in the broader context of future cities, what does it all add up to? It's easy to see the future as an overwhelming technological ecosystem, as complex and unwieldy as it is incomprehensible. I'm not going to say that this is not a possible outcome, particularly if we don't get a handle on issues such as climate change, but I see a potentially different picture—a simpler life. We tend to think that our grandparents generally led simpler lives than we do. There is no question that their daily commute was shorter, that people's days may have been marked by fewer interactions, if not more meaningful ones, and that there was no managing multiple social media profiles. Life may have been simpler in that there were fewer options and there was less information coming at us. But were we happier? That I don't know. What I do know is that today is exciting, fast-paced, and at times overwhelming. It feels like we have arrived at tomorrow with only half the tools we need to navigate the future. The irony in all of this technology and information, of course, is that we may be heading back to a much simpler time. I believe that a peer-to-peer social safety net could emerge over time, relieving government of its central role in the delivery of certain services while reintroducing the sense of community that we lost throughout the twentieth century along with our people-oriented streets.

Some of the questions I am leaving you with don't have easy answers. But just because there is uncertainty does not mean that there is not a road map for managing and shaping the future. Good managers always adjust to environmental changes around them, but use the same simple change management tools over and over while keeping a cup-half-full mentality. As with so many of the projects that I have undertaken over my career, we do not know all of the future funding mechanisms, models, or final outcomes, but that's okay. As successful organizations and individuals have been doing since the beginning of human existence, we can put our heads together and creatively figure it out. We can use strategies that have worked in different times and apply them to today's set of unique circumstances and opportunities. At a macro level, I think we need to do the same with the cities of the future. Think of it as the earth project, with a slew of messy subparts that need to be dissected and translated into manageable milestones that we must achieve for the sake of our cities and our lives.

I hope that I have stimulated some thought with regard to the potential that we face in the not too distant future, and how you can play a role in the change.

You can be the change, and knowledge is power. If you feel that you have a better sense directionally where we are headed, you can use that to free yourself from fear of the unknown. After all, unpredictability is inherently what makes cities exciting places to be, isn't it? So if you can accept the inherent entropy of the changes on the horizon, there is a better chance you can grab on and not just follow the trends, but actually help set a course for the future.

In the near future, social entrepreneurs in the public and private sectors will need to partner more than ever before for the sake of positive change and for the public good, rather than exploitive profiting. If they do so, I believe that there will be bigger financial returns and meaningful savings for all of us in the near term, much of it in the form of higher returns on our investments. Even more important, there will be triple-bottom-line profits with real societal progress in the medium to long term. This shift will require more open-minded people in positions of power, less dogma and more data, fewer fiefdoms, and instead a focus on customer satisfaction mated to selfless service. We also need to work harder to sell these benefits by taking the time to align incentives for our varied stakeholders first, which breeds long-term success and partnership. If we can achieve these partnerships, and the resulting benefits, we can leave a better place for our children. Now is the time for us to stretch our abilities and expectations, grab on to the change that is happening, and have the courage to push and mold that change for the greater good, even if it sometimes means a perception of "failure" in the short term. Only with that sense of fearlessness and risk-taking can we harness the best of what makes us human to forge a better future.

Acknowledgments

T he following people have taught me so much—some about life priorities, some about how to get things done. I want to thank you for all of your support over the years, and the laughter as we made change and had fun doing it, or in some cases just had fun.

Personal: To my dad (RIP), who always taught me the importance of humility and putting your life on the line for what's right and also how to make a dollar. To my mother, who taught me to always be right, and how to spend a dollar. Susan (and Bob!): Without you I would likely be in a ditch or jail, so I sort of owe being here and being functional to you. Lucan: It's been so important for me to grow up and get to know you and see that we have so many of the same problems (ha). Freya: You show me what it means to have an amazing work ethic—we can do this, ok? Todd: How to be a good person, and good on TV and radio—really good. You should be the one writing a book—on science! Tom: How to keep it street, and be savvy; one of the characters in the infographics may be you (the hipster-urban bank robber aesthetic). Con-Lons: How to keep your priorities straight and, yes, have it all! Richard: How to be real, loyal, and the always-on transportation entrepreneur. The Sisters: Perseverance, loyalty, and . . . that's it, friends for life! Luis & Tara: So happy for you guys, well deserved happiness. Sohnenbergs: How to party every night, drink the finest water, and not even spend one dollar. You will be awesome, slightly uptight parents. Kate: Amazing agrarian, and a good friend and person: Do you! Dr. Bippikopolous: Understated funniness is a virtue. AJ Stumpy Johnson, T-Bird, Christine, Dan, Anthony, and the whole Zipcar crew: Friends first, right? How to have maximum fun, creativity, and extreme organization at the same time: we did it. To all the musicians, artists, and comedians: You help us make it through and make life and our cities vibrant. Stephanie: You have taught me so many things, and none of this would be possible without your love and support. Thank you for being you. All of my other friends whom I don't have room to mention: Thank you.

The Biz: Thanks to Dan Tangherlini for seeing what others were scared of and being a great mentor. Adrian Fenty: You taught me real loyalty, that mistakes were OK in government, and how to put it on the line with no fear. Rahm Emanuel: How to be politically savvy, and get the job done, and be nicer than people think (Obamacare anyone?). Robin and Roy: Never be afraid to speak your mind, and take chances. Leah: Thanks for your loyalty, support, smarts, hard work, and ability to laugh when the chips are down. Scott: The same for you, and the ability to have a singular focus and get the painful stuff done against the odds. Harriet Tregoning: For welcoming me into government and being my partner in crime. Casey and Marc Willson, Joe, Jim, and the Bikes USA team: We worked so hard and learned so much, and fell in love with bikes all over again. Janette: It is a street fight sometimes and there is no room for losers; kudos. Tiger and the Go Pal team: Doing what you love for little money is still better than doing soulless work. Randy Neufeld, Lois Scott, John Tolva, and the Chicago heavyweights: How to make change against the odds. Zipcar management:

What a ride, huh? Who thought we would sell to Avis? My On The Fly partners and coworkers: You can create an entirely new category and business model and not make any money from it (Richard Branson also told me that about Virgin-Go). Terry, Karina, Nick, Tina, and the DDOT team: What an education we all got; thanks for working to make D.C. a shining national example on so many fronts. Luann, Janet, Dan, Taquanda, and the CDOT team: We got a tremendous amount done, fast, and the city will forever be better for it. To the amazing teams at Divvy and Capital Bikeshare. DOT: Ray LaHood, Polly, Beth, Peter, Joe, Victor, Sabrina, et al.: You were the best class. Thank you for all of your support. Chris Hamilton and the whole Arlington team for setting great examples for all of us. ULI and Patrick and Jess: I should have done the full year! What an amazing experience. Thanks NACTO team for your support, collaboration, and hard, sometimes thankless, work to make cities better. Janette, Linda, David, Corinne, Skye, and Matt. Martha and the Green Lane Project: You made a huge difference and continue to for cities around the country. To all of my social entrepreneur start-ups: You are changing the world every day and I am proud to stand with all of you. Fontinalis team: We are just beginning and will change the world for the better. To all the organizations, advocates, and activists that have supported our work—Rockefeller Foundation, Open Plans, Streetsblog, Streetfilms (Clarence!), Active Transportation Alliance, Washington Area Bicyclists Association, Coalition for Smarter Growth, *Greater Greater Washington,* and the individuals who fight for better cities and safer streets every day in cities all around the world.

This book: Thanks to Heather Boyer from Island Press for spending more than a year discussing *Start-Up City* and then putting up with David and me as we worked our way through it. David, for working on this while going through MIT; that was crazy. Kate Chanba, you dove in and helped us get it done, thank you. The entire Island Press team: muchas gracias.

Knight Foundation: Carol Coletta and Benjie de la Peña, you all are the best, and without your support, and that of Alberto and Knight, this project would not have happened. I hope *Start-Up City* helps to give a road map to aspiring urban disrupters to make the change that we know so desperately needs to happen, and helps in any small way to give the great people out there who need it a push to help to make our cities great, from wherever they sit.

Thanks to you for reading *Start-Up City*. Now let's go get sh*t done. There is no time to waste.

That's a wrap.

Gabe Klein was born in Hartford, Connecticut. He started working in his father's bicycle shop at the age of five and has had a lifelong love affair with transportation as a result. After moving to rural Virginia at the age of ten to go to a yoga school on an ashram, Gabe went on to study business in college with a vision to create change via commerce. He continued to cut his teeth in the retail bicycle business for a number of years in Washington, D.C., and Florida, then worked in various technology-oriented startups before meeting Robin Chase at Zipcar in 2002. Robin hired him as the vice president for the D.C. region for the nascent startup. Following his four years at Zipcar, Gabe went on to write a business model for the first point-to-point car sharing concept with Richard Branson's Virgin Group.

He then cofounded On The Fly, the first all-natural, electric-powered multi-unit food truck company in the United States back in 2007. Gabe then became the director of the Washington, D.C. Department of Transportation under Mayor Adrian Fenty at the beginning of 2009, where he reinvented the agency with a focus on customer service, technology, and active transportation, including the launch of Capital Bikeshare, the first large-scale bike-share system in the United States. At the end of Adrian Fenty's term, Rahm Emanuel hired Gabe to hit the reset button on the Chicago DOT and build one hundred miles of advanced bike lanes, design and build the Chicago Riverwalk and the Bloomingdale Trail, and launch the largest bike-share system in the United States—Divvy. In 2015, Gabe is once again a social entrepreneur and assists a portfolio of technology and mobility companies that share his values, is a special venture partner at Fontinalis Partners in Detroit, which was cofounded by Bill Ford, and is happily raising his daughter Simone with his wife Stephanie in Columbia Heights in Washington, D.C.

David Vega-Barachowitz is an urban planner and designer based in New York City. From 2011 to 2014, he led the National Association of City Transportation Officials' (NACTO) efforts to compose new city street design codes and standards, while leading a peer-to-peer network of planning and transportation professionals from around North America. He is the coauthor of the NACTO *Urban Street Design Guide* and served as project manager for the *Urban Bikeway Design Guide*. He is currently pursuing his master's in city planning at the Massachusetts Institute of Technology.